READ ME LIKE A BOOK

Read Me Like a Book

*Using Hermeneutics as a Guide
to Pastoral Counseling*

JASON CUSICK

WIPF & STOCK · Eugene, Oregon

READ ME LIKE A BOOK
Using Hermeneutics as a Guide to Pastoral Counseling

Wipf & Stock
An Imprint of Wipf and Stock Publishers
199 W. 8th Ave., Suite 3
Eugene, OR 97401

www.wipfandstock.com

ISBN 13: 978-1-62564-146-5

Manufactured in the U.S.A.

To Asa, Ethan, and Elia.
You have refueled my curiosity for Scripture and people.

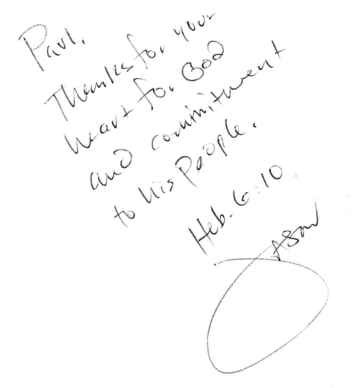

Paul,
Thanks for your
heart for God
and commitment
to his people.
Heb. 6:10

Jason

Contents

Preface   *ix*

Acknowledgments   *xiii*

Introduction: Reading Human Documents   1

1   Who Am I?
     The Pre-Understanding of the Interpreter   13

2   What Do You Mean?
     Listening for Authorial Intention   33

3   Can I Get Some Background?
     History, Culture, and Circumstantial Context   53

4   What Is the Big Idea?
     Interpreting Narrative Genre   71

5   What Do We Do Now?
     Finding Meaning-full Applications   91

     Final Thoughts: Exegeting People   111

     Appendix: A Quick Reference Guide for Pastors   117

     Bibliography   119

Preface

I HAVE ALWAYS WRESTLED with the relationship between the Bible and counseling. I have an undergraduate degree in Behavioral Sciences and worked for years in clinical chaplaincy. I have seen firsthand the effectiveness of psychology and professional counseling for believers and non-believers alike. But I am also a pastor with graduate and postgraduate degrees in Christian ministry, leadership, and preaching. I have worked in the local church and believe in the transforming power of God's Word and Christian discipleship.

Like many evangelicals, I have moved in and out of two "camps" regarding the relationship between the Bible and counseling. For a time I was an "integrationist," believing that we could harvest the best of the Bible and psychology in helping to shepherd God's people, but I struggled to find a clear methodology for how to draw from these two areas with consistent integrity. I then moved toward a "Bible only" approach, wanting my pastoral counseling to be more grounded in discipleship and obedience, but I regularly encountered the need to explore thoughts, experiences, and feelings that the Bible did not explicitly address. When the "spiritual formation" movement began to increase in popularity, I thought it might provide the bridge between counseling and the Bible I was looking for, but the movement felt more like an evangelical experiment in historical spirituality than a sound theoretical approach I could use in my daily pastoral ministry.

One day while immersed in reading, I noticed that my books on counseling and my books on hermeneutics included some of the same names in the footnotes; names like Paul Ricoeur,

E. D. Hirsch, and Hans-Georg Gadamer. I wondered why exegetes and counselors alike were citing the same seminal writers and source materials. Following my curiosity, I discovered that experts in counseling psychology and experts in hermeneutics and homiletics share much in common. They are all part of a broad field of study: "interpretation." As I dug deeper into "interpretation theory," the words of one pastoral theologian helped me see the connection between the Bible and counseling. Anton Boisen, the founder of the Clinical Pastoral Education movement, referred to people as "living human documents."[1] When I read those words, something clicked. I asked myself: "What if pastors studying Scripture and counselors helping people are really doing the same thing? What if they are both trying to understand two different kinds of documents—written and human? Is it possible that the same set of skills used to read written documents (hermeneutics) could be used to read human documents (pastoral counseling)?"

This book was written because I am a pastor who needs practical tools to help hurting people. I have to balance my time between preaching and counseling. These two ministries sometimes feel worlds apart. This book attempts to bring the idea of "reading people like books" one step closer to pastors in the trenches. I believe the field of psychology has much to offer and I have been personally blessed by the ministry many professional Christian therapists, but we pastors have a wealth of untapped resources in our own theological library.

The connection between pastoral counseling and hermeneutics has been there for years. In many ways, I am harvesting the hard work of many skilled laborers to assemble a more digestible meal for those of us with limited time to eat. I am particularly indebted Donald Capps, Charles Gerkin, and Anthony Thiselton, pastoral theologians who have done much of the "theoretical heavy lifting" when it comes to understanding Ricoeur, Hirsch, Boisen, and others who have explored the relationship between interpretation theory, counseling, and pastoral ministry. My hope is that this book will provide you with a practical, hermeneutically-based

---

1. Boisen, "Living Human Document," 22.

approach to counseling that will inspire you to re-read your hermeneutics and homiletics books with new eyes, seeing them anew as resources that will help you better understand both Scripture and people.

Acknowledgments

My humble thanks to Rex Johnson and Kent Edwards, two professors who helped me reconcile pastoral counseling and preaching. You have guided my thinking, encouraged my devotional life, and reminded me that my most important calling is my marriage, not my ministry.

To my friend Donald Capps, who has encouraged me for close to ten years through his emails, letters, and phone calls. Don is a pillar in the field of pastoral theology. Your insights, encouragement, and prayers have enriched me.

To my counselor, who has helped my unpack my pre-understanding, deliberate over my core beliefs, question my assumptions, and helped me apply the "Big Ideas" of my life in so many ways through the last few years. My soul thanks you.

To Marie, my wonderful wife, you give me space to create because you believe in me and also because you know how annoying and irritable I am when I am not writing. And no, you don't have to read this book either. You've heard it all already. I love you.

To Christian Amondson, Matthew Wimer, Alex Fus, Patrick Harrison, and the team at Wipf and Stock, thank you for seeing the value in this book and your grace in making it come to life. May this book help create new discussion that enables pastors to grow in their understanding of Scripture and people.

In God's service . . . and yours.

Introduction

Reading Human Documents

As the new pastor of Community Christian Church, the first six months of ministry were not what Dan had expected. Dan was hired because his seminary education had placed a heavy emphasis on exegesis and homiletics and the congregation lacked strong biblical teaching on Sunday mornings. He looked forward to serving a church that valued expository preaching. Nothing excited him more than digging into the text, finding the timeless truths of Scripture, and passionately communicating them to people looking for God's direction in their lives. But by the end of his first month at the church, Dan was feeling discouraged. He wasn't prepared for all the pastoral care and counseling needs of the congregation. He called a friend who was a pastor in a neighboring city.

"It feels like every time I sit down to start my exegesis, I get another call from someone in crisis," Dan complained.

"Yeah," his friend replied, "I'm going through the same thing. I want to preach, but all these people's lives are falling apart."

"I can't even balance the time," Dan said, "But you know what the hardest part is? Counseling is so . . . different. It's like I have to totally shift gears."

"I know what you mean," his friend agreed.

"I feel like I'm doing some in-depth studying," Dan explained, "then somebody needs to meet with me and it's like that 'screeching to a stop' sound in my head. I'm not a counselor—I'm a preacher. I have a hard time just sitting and listening, trying to understand what someone is saying. Give me a text and I know what to do with it!"

"It feels so different to me too," his friend said. "I like to think I'm doing some of my best counseling when I'm preaching. It's the one-on-one thing that I'm not good at."

"Maybe I need to take some counseling classes or something," Dan wondered.

"Do you have time to do that?"

"No, I'm still trying to find time to finish studying for this sermon and my mid-week Bible study."

After the call, Dan sat quietly in his office. His next counseling appointment was waiting outside. He wondered if there was another way to help people. He cared about people, but felt more gifted at studying and preaching texts than pastoral counseling. He looked at the door. There was no time for sermon preparation. Dan was being called to minister to a hurting person. He closed his book and opened the door.

The Pastor's Dilemma

Pastors feel conflicted. We love to preach, teach, and study Scripture. We believe the best way for people to be comforted, strengthened, encouraged, and directed in life is by helping them understand and apply God's Word. Most of our seminary classes focused on hermeneutics, biblical languages, exegesis, and preaching. We feel called to "correctly handle the word of truth" (2 Tim 2:15), but when we begin pastoral ministry in the church, we are immediately sought out for pastoral counseling—something for which most us feel ill-equipped.

> . . . *when we begin pastoral ministry in the church, we are immediately sought out for pastoral counseling—something for which most us feel ill-equipped.*

The care needs in churches are overwhelming. Pastors are inundated with congregants suffering in the throes of grief, abuse, addiction, health changes, painful divorces, vocational confusion, parenting challenges, and a wide variety of other struggles. Research shows that "although some clergy acknowledge it was their own decision to complete seminary training without having a pastoral care course, up to 90 percent state they feel they were not adequately trained in seminary to cope with pastoral care needs in their congregation."[1] We pastors don't feel properly trained and we don't have the time! With elder meetings, church business, and sermon preparation, how can we "shift gears" to become counselors to people who are hurting? Our dilemma is that we feel torn between our passion for understanding Scripture and the call to care for hurting people. Pastors try to solve this dilemma in a different ways.

Attempted Solution 1: Refer to Another Person

"There *must* be someone else more qualified to handle these issues."

It is true that professional Christian therapists are a great resource for pastors. They have extensive training, available time, and can offer a different perspective to personal struggles. The problem with this seeming-solution is that people come to pastors for a reason. Pastors occupy a unique role that Christian therapists simply cannot fill. Another option is referring these hurting people to another pastor on staff, but most pastors will spend the majority of their ministry in what are called "pastoral churches" of fifty to 150 people. These churches are usually led by a solo pastor and rely heavily on that pastor for their care and counseling needs. Even training a team of pastoral care volunteers will still result in the "Moses Effect," for while volunteers may handle easier cases, more complicated counseling matters will still come to the pastor (Exod 18:25–26).

1. Ferguson, "Clergy Compassion Fatigue," 16–17.

Attempted Solution 2: Use Bible-Only Counseling

> "The Bible is all we need to help people with the problems they face in life."

Based on their strong convictions on the sufficiency of Scripture (2 Tim 3:16–17), some pastors believe the Bible is the only resource to use when helping hurting people. Out of a desire to stay away from secular psychology and worldly techniques, these pastors look for a solution clearly rooted in the centrality of Scripture. The problem with this attempted solution is that it is often poorly operationalized. Pastors compile and draw upon resources from discipleship methods, topical Bible references, and prayer ministries, but the underlying theoretical approach is usually haphazard. And even those pastors who want nothing to do with modern psychology often use research and techniques borrowed from or influenced by secular psychology.[2] While Bible-only counseling has much to offer, it is often missing important components necessary for accurate assessment and treatment of people's deep hurts and struggles.

Attempted Solution 3: Learn Psychological-Counseling Techniques

> "We should take some lessons from professional therapists."

Seeing the effectiveness of professional counselors, some pastors read books, take classes, and attend seminars taught by professional psychologists. The problem here is that pastors often find this attempted solution to be more confusing than helpful. Charles Kollar writes, "When a minister reads a book on counseling, he often feels like a fish out of water. How is he going to find the time to use these theories properly? Many feel the frustration of having little to build on because their foundation for teaching and training

---

2. Mack, "Developing a Helping Relationship," 181.

is through faith, Scripture, and the church."[3] For want of "integration" of counseling and the Bible, pastors end up doing little more than cherry-picking ideas from therapists without any solid theory of how to combine therapeutic techniques and pastoral ministry.

How can pastors fully give themselves over to the study of Scripture and sermon preparation, even while they seek to become more effective in their pastoral care and counseling? The answer to this dilemma is found in the field of interpretation.

Leveraging Your Interpretative Skills

Pastors are better equipped for pastoral care and counseling than they realize. Hermeneutics, exegesis, homiletics, pastoral care, and counseling all have a common foundation in the broad field of interpretation. The question is not, "Is there a relationship between Scripture study, sermon preparation, pastoral care and counseling?" The question is, "What is the relationship?"

In 1925, a religious educator named Anton Boisen was helping seminarians under his tutelage to gain pastoral experience. He wanted them to have first-hand knowledge of human nature, so he assigned them to visit patients at a nearby hospital. Recognizing that his students had more interest in studying Scripture than in caring for people directly, Boisen encouraged them to see the patients as "living human documents." This idea is the solution to the pastor's dilemma: People are like books!

Pastors can apply their understanding and practice of exegesis to the ministries of pastoral care and counseling by learning to *interpret people as they interpret Scripture.* Charles Gerkin writes, "Persons seek out a pastoral counselor because they need someone to listen to their story . . . The story itself is, of course, an interpretation of experience. To seek counseling usually means that the interpretation has become painful, the emotions evoked by the interpretation powerful and conflicted. The search is for a

---

3. Kollar, *Solution-Focused Pastoral Counseling,* 22.

listener who is an expert at interpretation."[4] People come to counseling looking for an "expert at interpretation." This is the pastor's calling! We are gifted and passionate about interpretation. By leveraging our skills in hermeneutics, exegesis, and homiletics we can increase our competence and confidence in our pastoral care and counseling.

To interpret is to explain the meaning of something, understand its significance, or translate it into a new way of understanding. Some of us interpret certain things better than others. This is what Jesus noticed about the religious leaders of his day. He criticized these leaders for being able to interpret some things, but not others. He said, "You know how to interpret the appearance of the sky, but you cannot interpret the signs of the times?" (Matt 16:1–3). Living in an agricultural society, these people were good as understanding the weather, but they were spiritually clueless. Jesus wanted them to leverage their ability to interpret the weather and apply it to spirituality.

> *By leveraging our skills in hermeneutics, exegesis, and homiletics we can increase our competence and confidence in our pastoral care and counseling.*

The Bible has a lot to say about the act of interpretation. Consider the following Hebrew and Greek words that are variously used for "interpretation" in the Bible:

- פשר (*peshar*) a solution to a puzzle or problem (Eccl 8:1)

- הבין (*habin*) understanding (Prov 1:6)

- μεθερμηνευω (*methermeneuo*) translation (Mark 15:22, 34)

- διακρινω (*diakrino*) learning by discrimination, deciding (Matt 16:1–3)

- επιλυσις (*epilysis*) explanation (2 Pet 1:20)

4. Gerkin, *Living Human Document*, 26.

These same words describe what happens when someone comes to us for care and counseling. Hurting people seek counseling when they are looking for a solution to a problem in life. They want understanding. They want an explanation for the situation in which they find themselves. Sometimes people want to have their thoughts and feelings translated into words they can understand. Counseling demands decision-making, discernment, and the ability to separate larger issues into manageable problems. It involves helping people locate an explanation for what is happening to them or find where God is in their hurts and struggles.

Interpretation skills are not rooted in the Bible or psychology. They are part of the much larger field of epistemology, the study of how we know things. In interpretation, we draw from a wide variety of disciplines such as philosophy, logic, semantics, communication theory, and ethnography. Even the most conservative biblical scholars, who claim that Bible alone is sufficient to help people, draw from these fields in order to interpret the Bible itself! Whether we are studying the Bible or counseling a hurting person, we are using the skills of interpretation.

> *Whether we are studying the Bible or counseling a hurting person, we are using the skills of interpretation.*

Bible interpretation and pastoring counseling need no longer be seen as competing for our time. They are intimately connected. As Tim Keller reminds us, "It's a great mistake to pit pastoral care . . . against preaching preparation. It is only through working with people that you become the preacher you need to be—someone who knows sin, how the heart works, what people's struggles are, and so on. To some degree, pastoral care and leadership *are* sermon preparation! They prepare the preacher and not just the sermon."[5]

Gerkin asks, "Does the image of the person . . . as a living human document open to us a possible way of approaching the task of restoring pastoral counseling to a sense of its mission and

---

5. Keller, "How He Prepares Sermons," http://www.preachingtoday.com/skills/2009/november/timkelleronhowhepreparessermons.html.

purpose defined theologically?"[6] The answer is yes. Studying the Bible and counseling people are more similar than they are different. As we grow in our ability to interpret the Bible, we can leverage those skills to improve our ability to care for hurting people. At their core, biblical interpretation and pastoral counseling both involve the same basic interpretive questions.

The Five Questions

Below are five questions that can guide us in providing effective pastoral care and counseling to hurting people. These correspond to what I call the "Five Steps of Interpretation" in hermeneutics and homiletics (which include pre-understanding, authorial intent, context, genre, and application).

1. Who Am I?

What we know, how we feel, what we believe, and how we make decisions impacts how we interpret new information. In what ways does interpreting the Bible and people start with an honest self-understanding?

2. What Do You Mean?

Words, phrases, and ideas have different meanings to different people. How can we learn to listen to and understand what a text or person is trying to say rather than assuming we already know what something means?

3. Can I Get Some Background?

Culture, history, and other background information are sometimes the key to interpretation. How can we look behind what is

---

6. Gerkin, *Living Human Document*, 39.

written or said to understand the important issues that lie beneath the surface?

4. What's the Big Idea?

Our lives, like the Bible, are filled with stories. Stories involve character, plot, conflict, and resolution. How can understanding the main idea of a story help us make sense of it and know what to do with it?

5. What Do We Do Now?

We want change. Using our interpretative skills should lead us to see things in new ways. How does proper interpretation guide us toward practical life changes?

The first three steps (and chapters of this book) focus on listening, asking questions, and collecting information. Whether we are studying a text or counseling a person, I believe these three steps take up 50 to 70 percent of our interpretative time. The last two steps (and chapters) focus on working with people to draw out the main issues they are facing and help them create action plans to address these problems. Each chapter of this book will explore how these questions relate to biblical interpretation and counseling hurting people. I have also included questions, examples, exercises, and recommended readings to explore these ideas in greater depth. Pastors will find insights that will help them reconcile the seemingly different ministries of hermeneutics and pastoral counseling. Counselors will find connections between their work and the field of biblical interpretation. And my hope is that we will all discover basic principles to help us understand Scripture and understand people.

If there is one thing that hermeneutics and counseling have in common, it is that both require a delicate balance of skill and inspiration. Interpretation is done with the head as well as the heart. Whether we are trying to understand the Bible or the story of a hurting person, we must understand theory even as we open ourselves to the movement of the Holy Spirit, always remembering that hermeneutics is:

> . . . neither an art nor a science; it is both a science and an art. We use rules, principles, methods, and tactics; we enter the worlds of the historian, sociologist, psychologist, and linguist—to name a few. Yet, human communication cannot be reduced solely to quantifiable and precise rules. No mechanical system of rules will ever help one understand correctly all the implications or nuances in the three words "I love you" as spoken by a teenage girl to her boyfriend, a husband to a wife of twenty-five years, a mother to her child, or a teenage boy to his mint-condition '54 Chevy. This is where the "art" of interpretation enters in.[7]

Recommended Reading

Pastoral Care in the Small Membership Church by James L. Killen, Jr.

> This book is aimed at solo pastors and highlights the opportunities and challenges of doing ministry in "pastoral churches" in which the pastor is heavily relied upon for pastoral care and counseling.

Foundations of Pastoral Care by Bruce Petersen

> This is a comprehensive and historical look at pastoral care in the church. Both readable and practical, it emphasizes the

7. Klein et al., *Introduction to Bible Interpretation*, 5.

role of the pastor as well as detailing how care can be provided through laity and small groups.

Caring for Souls: Counseling under the Authority of Scripture by Harry Shields and Gary J. Bredfeldt

This work offers a thoughtful and highly applicable resource for pastors wrestling with the relationship between the Bible and counseling. The authors trace the Bible versus counseling debate back to similar philosophical and theological debates in church history.

1

Who Am I?

The Pre-Understanding of the Interpreter

What we know, how we feel, what we believe, and how we make decisions impact how we interpret new information. In what ways does interpreting the Bible and people start with an honest self-understanding?

PASTOR DAN OPENED THE door of his office and invited Sarah to come in. She was a causally dressed woman in her late forties, slightly shorter than Dan, and carried what seemed to Dan to be an unusually large purse. She didn't look upset. She sat down across from Dan, set her purse on the floor next to her chair, turned off her cell phone, and looked up.

"Thank you for meeting with me today, Pastor," she began. "I won't take much of your time. Before we start, I don't think I've ever sat down and talked to a pastor before about, you know, things in my life. I've been coming to the church for a while now . . . off and on, but not as often as I should. I was raised Catholic and didn't go to Mass every week, so I guess it's hard to get into the habit of coming every week."

She shifted in her chair and rolled her eyes. "I don't know why I said all that. But I guess you are my pastor . . . Anyway. I'm married. This is my second marriage. My husband is an engineer. We have three teenage sons. I homeschool all of them. That's kind of a juggling act right now," she sighs. "But the main reason I came to see you today is that since my brother's death, my faith doesn't seem as strong as it used to be."

Pastor Dan's mind was already filled with thoughts and questions. She was nominally raised Catholic, he thought to himself. Why the change to this church? Is she saved or seeking? She considers me to be her pastor? What does "pastor" mean to her? And her second marriage? Is she widowed? Divorced? I wonder what happened. Married to an engineer . . . Homeschooling mom . . . Teenage sons . . . God bless her! Brother died. What happened? What's going on with her faith since this loss?

Sarah's words also triggered some of Dan's own feelings convictions. He thought, I grew up Catholic and I really have a heart for Catholics looking for Jesus. You say you love the music, but what about my teaching every week? I just counseled a couple struggling in their second marriage—not another one! That homeschooling group has really been pushing me about preaching homeschooling from the pulpit. Is Sarah part of that group? Her brother died. That's really close to home. I still don't think I'm over my sister's death.

Dan's racing thoughts remind us that before the person we are listening to completes a sentence or even begins to speak, our own knowledge, attitudes, beliefs, and approaches to problem-solving are already at work. This is called pre-understanding. It is the first step of interpretation.

What Is Pre-Understanding?

We don't come to interpretation as blank slates. Our previous education and experiences affect how we interpret what see, hear, and read. Whether the document is written or human, our pre-understanding shapes our interpretation. In a very practical sense, interpretation begins with the interpreter in four areas:[1]

1. What I Know

What information do I already possess about the subject I am interpreting? Is this a new area of study for which I have little or no information? In regards to biblical interpretation: Have I studied this Bible passage before? Am I familiar with this genre? Do I know the history and culture of the time? In regards to pastoral counseling: Have I counseled this person before or someone similar? Am I familiar with the general issue this person is facing? Is there any important information I need which I currently do not have?

2. How I Feel

What are the feelings I have about the subject I am interpreting? In what ways will my mood (positively or negatively) impact my interpretation? Regarding biblical interpretation: Is this passage of Scripture exciting or a burden? Will this text cause unwanted reactions from the congregation? Is this a subject I preach on regularly because I am so passionate about it? With regard to pastoral counseling: How do I feel about the person I am counseling? Is the session interesting or boring, life-giving or annoying? Do I feel hurried, tired, restless, or frustrated for some reason?

3. What I Believe

What theological, moral, political, or philosophical views do I possess that shape my interpretation? In what ways is my worldview predetermining how I read a text or person? In regards to biblical interpretation: Am I Calvinistic, Arminian, Dispensational, Covenantal, or Reformed? Am I a Cessationist or Continuationist? Am I Complementarian or Egalitarian? Regarding pastoral counseling:

1. Ferguson, *Biblical Hermenuetics, 13.*

Is addiction to be considered a sin or a disease? How do people grieve properly? What do I believe about marriage, divorce, and remarriage? What are my views on parenting or aging?

4. How I Decide

What is my cognitive style? What is my methodology when it comes to thinking through issues? With regards to biblical interpretation: Am I inductive or deductive? Am I linear or non-linear? Are the first questions I ask historical/scientific or literary/narrative? In regards to pastoral counseling: Is my process slower and relational or more diagnostic and problem-solution oriented? Do I quote Scripture or try to draw Scripture from the people I am counseling? Do I see people as individuals or as part of larger systems and families?

Our pre-understanding is like a storehouse. We draw from it to know what to ask and what we need not ask. It guides our thinking process and shapes how we make sense of what we are learning. Our pre-understanding comes from our education, but is also formed and shaped by our spiritual giftedness, personality, vocational experience, cultural background, family dynamics, religious upbringing, successes and failures, and a variety of other sources. We bring this storehouse to the interpretive act.

> *Our pre-understanding is like a storehouse. We draw from it to know what to ask and what we need not ask. It guides our thinking process and shapes how we make sense of what we are learning.*

It is important to note that our pre-understanding should not be the basis for our interpretation. It is important and necessary, but also comes with its problems. "Our pre-understanding is our friend, not our enemy. It provides a set of understandings by which we can make sense of what we read. The problem is that our pre-understanding too easily becomes prejudice . . . The reader's background and ideas are important in the study of biblical truth; however, this must be used to study meaning rather than create meaning that is not there."[2]

Is My Pre-Understanding Helping or Harming?

Our pre-understanding is like a reflex. When we read, see, or hear something, we react based on who we are and what we know. Sometimes this reflex is helpful. The Bible tells a story of a Roman soldier who came to Jesus asking him to heal his bedridden servant. When Jesus offered to go to the house, the solider stopped him and said, "Lord, I do not deserve to have you come under my roof. But just say the word, and my servant will be healed. For I myself am a man under authority, with soldiers under me. I tell this one, 'Go,' and he goes; and that one, 'Come,' and he comes. I say to my servant, 'Do this,' and he does it" (Matt 8:8–9). The soldier's military experience taught him that powerful people make things happen in ways the rest of us can't. This soldier's pre-understanding aided in him making sense of what was in front of him.

A few years ago, I was listening to my pastor talk about his research trip to Egypt. He visited the Temple of Hathor, an ancient Egyptian god represented as a cow. My pastor described how he had learned that worshippers would scrape the temple walls with a rock, collect the shavings, put them in water, and drink it. It sounded like a very strange practice, but also struck me as oddly familiar. Then my pre-understanding kicked into gear. I remembered a story from the Book of Exodus in which Moses came down from the mountain after receiving the Ten Commandments. He saw Israelites worshipping a golden calf, and infuriated by their idolatry, Moses "took the calf they had made, burned it up, and ground it to powder. He scattered the powder over the surface of the water and forced the Israelites to drink the water" (Exod 32:20). Was Hathor the golden calf they were worshipping? Maybe Moses

2. Osborne, *Hermeneutical Spiral*, 29.

was saying, "If you want to worship Hathor, then go all the way in your idolatry!" My previous knowledge of the Exodus story helped me interpret this new information, expanding the storehouse of my pre-understanding in the process.

As helpful as it often is, our pre-understanding can also lead us in the wrong direction. Job, the righteous patriarch of the Old Testament, sought the help of his friends in his suffering. Unfortunately, Job's friends had only one way of understanding suffering—as a punishment from God. Eliphaz insisted that Job was getting what he deserved (Job 4:7–9, 11:5–6), while Bildad believed that a true confession of sin would reverse Job's suffering (Job 8:3–7), and Zophar agreed with the others in believing that God had been merciful enough with Job (Job 11:4–6, 14–15)! Their education and experience caused them to misinterpret the situation. Charles Kraft argues, "we learn as part of our cultural conditioning a set of 'interpretational reflexes'—a set of habits in terms of which we automatically interpret whatever happens . . . we need to develop hermeneutical techniques for getting beyond these reflexive interpretations."[3]

I am reminded of an instance when I was working with a family dealing with Alzheimer's disease. One day I got a call from the husband. His wife was suffering an episode and didn't recognize him. I encouraged him to find their wedding photo album and try to convince her that they were married. Faithfully trusting his pastor, he followed my suggestions, but it didn't help. His wife became increasingly frustrated as more of my suggestions did little to help. I spoke with her over the phone and tried to talk her into believing he was her husband. It was futile. The problem was my pre-understanding. I had limited information about Alzheimer's disease. After meeting privately with a social worker with expertise in this area and reading a Christian book on the subject, I learned that someone with Alzheimer's simply cannot be talked out of an episode like this. There are other ways to help them, like focusing on their feelings, redirecting their attention, or reevaluating their medications. This is what makes this disease so painful and

---

3. Kraft, *Christianity in Culture*, 102.

exhausting for caregivers. A limited or flawed pre-understanding can result in ineffective and possibly harmful ministry.

Are You "Drawing from" or "Reading into"?

"Exegesis" refers to the critical explanation or interpretation of a text. It comes from a Greek word meaning "to draw out." Sound principles of biblical exegesis include looking for the author's original intention, exploring important cultural and historical contextual information, considering the literary genre of the author, and seeking relevant modern-day applications for the meaning of the text. The opposite of exegesis is "eisegesis." Coming from a Greek word meaning "into," eisegesis refers to the process of interpreting a text in such a way that one's own presuppositions, agendas, and biases are brought into or placed onto the text. Considering our pre-understanding is important because at any point in the hermeneutical process, we can be tempted to inappropriately "read into" the text from our own pre-understanding.

> *... at any point in the hermeneutical process, we can be tempted to inappropriately "read into" the text from our own pre-understanding.*

We choose to study or preach a text for specific reasons. Though we seek to make the author's intention our priority, our own intentions are ever before us. We emphasize one part of a given passage more than another. We often feel we relate to the original author in certain ways and may imagine our own thoughts in their heads. In looking at culture and history, we may overlook certain information, believing that we understand it well enough already. We are inclined toward only certain kinds of literature. We may create applications of Scripture that are too close to our own agendas and exclude other applications altogether. In many circumstances, the role of our pre-understanding is a natural and normal part of the exegetical process.

In the worst-case scenarios, our pre-understanding runs amok. We make Scripture say things the author never intended. We completely ignore the importance of history, culture, and context. We take a story from the Bible and use it to illustrate what we want to teach, which is sometimes the very opposite of what God is communicating in the passage. We neglect applications or create applications that don't in any way relate to the meaning of the text. We are all sometimes guilty of eisegesis, or "reading into" Scripture when studying a passage or preparing a sermon. It is an occupational hazard that comes with time constraints, pressures, laziness, pastoral agendas, and the complicated task of finding the modern relevance of ancient texts.

Are You Transferring Your Baggage?

Eisegesis is indeed an occupational hazard in pastoral care and counseling. When someone comes to us for counseling, we may be preoccupied with sermon preparation, budget planning, other church business, or concerns at home. As we counsel, we selectively listen. We relate to some parts of a person's story and ignore other elements. As we listen, we are already scanning a concordance in our mind of passages of Scripture that could help address the person's problem. Sometimes a person's hurts remind us of our own hurts and we begin to get strong feelings about what we are hearing. When we decide to speak, advise, and share our thoughts, we speak from our own interpretation. We may appear to be doing strategic pastoral counseling, but if our personal baggage has influenced us in the wrong way, our counseling may be more eisegetical than exegetical.

> *A counselor or pastor will always be faced with the "temptation to work on his or her own problems during the counseling session."*

One example of how this plays out is through what is called counter-transference. Counter-transference is when a counselor transfers his or her personal feelings onto the person they want to help. This usually stems from unresolved issues in the life of the counselor or pastor. A counselor or pastor will always be faced with the "temptation to work on his or her own problems during the counseling session."[4] For example, during a recent counseling session, a man in his fifties was questioning his current job and considering retirement. He was feeling frustrated by the lack of clarity in his life and even more frustrated by what he sensed was God's silence on the issue. As he spoke, his voice rose in volume and he began ask me a series of pointed questions about God's will and my opinion. As his emotions changed, so did mine. I went from being open and empathetic to protective and angry. I wanted to stop him from what felt like a barrage of questions. I started to feel attacked. I felt like the questions were designed to test me to prove I was smart enough to be a pastor. When he pointed his finger at me while asking one particularly accusatory question, I had had enough. I directed him to a career counselor, prayed for him, and quickly wrapped up the appointment. Later, when talking to a mentor, I realized that counter-transference had occurred. The man's loud, impassioned series of questions reminded me of a very controlling and insecure relative of mine whose questions are usually disguised manipulations and accusations. In such times, I normally get very upset or retreat in silence. So it was that during what seemed like a normal pastoral counseling session, my emotional baggage got mixed up with his emotional baggage.

Counter-transference happens on the level of feelings, not of thinking. When it happens, we are no longer interacting with the person in front of us; we are interacting with our own thoughts, feelings, and personal wounds. Imagine providing pastoral counseling to someone that reminds you of your abusive ex-husband, or the boy your daughter ran away with, or your childhood bully. Anything can trigger this transfer of feelings—the counselee's personality, attitude, life circumstance, or even their voice. When this happens, we begin "reading into," rather than "drawing out."

---

4. Petersen, *Foundations of Pastoral Care*, 107.

The transfer of feelings can also happen when counselees transfer their unresolved feelings into us. This is called transference. For example, a young woman once came to meet with me about feeling disconnected with God. I listened to her struggles and provided some sensitive guidance. She seemed very thankful, more thankful than I expected. She then confided that her father had died when she was a teenager. She told me how soft-spoken and thoughtful he was—just like me. I realized that there was potentially some transference happening. The young woman eventually worked through her struggles with God and I have not seen her for counseling since. God may have in some strange way used the transference to help her feel accepted. But if we are not careful, transference can open doors of temptation, boundary problems, and eventually even sin.

We cannot completely avoid transference and counter-transference any more than we can avoid our pre-understanding's influence on interpretation. The question we must ask ourselves is, "Am I aware of what is going on inside of me as I am interpreting these documents, written or human?" We must be aware of the important role our pre-understanding plays in the interpretive process.

Pre-Understanding in Pastoral Counseling

1. Inventory and Enhance Your Storehouse

On a recent airline flight, I overhead a man talking about his possessions back home: "I've got a storage unit twice the size of my garage," he laughed, "and I don't even know what's in there anymore!" That's how many of us relate to our pre-understanding. We have a lot stored, but we are often not sure of what's there or how it affects our interpretation. The most effective pastors are attuned to their pre-understanding. They are intentional in their learning, diverse in their reading, aware of their faults and blind spots, and continually reflect on the lessons they have learned through experience.

Each of has a storehouse of pre-understanding that includes information, feelings, beliefs, and approaches to decision-making.

My pre-understanding includes the following influences: Southern California native, father died when I was eleven, youngest son, interracial/Asian spouse, came to Christ in college, discipled in an African-American church, evangelical, hospital chaplain, twelve-step background, writer, movie buff, politically ambiguous, heterosexual, psychology degree, workaholic and detail-oriented, analytical, progressive dispensationalist, professional ministry in a mega-church, etc. All of these factors and more contribute to my interpretative process. What is in your storehouse?

Take time to inventory your storehouse. Ask yourself the following questions: On what topics do I have a lot of knowledge or confidence? About what issues do I have very strong feelings (either positive and negative)? How would I describe my theological, political, and ideological look on life? How would I describe how I process information and problem-solve? How would I describe my personality? What significant experiences have I had in my life (both positive and negative) and what effect do I believe these memories have on how I interpret God, people, and the world? What are my spiritual gifts, natural talents, and strengths?

Inventory is just the beginning. To better understand the Bible and people, we must enhance our storehouse. Robert McKee teaches story development and genre to entertainment industry professionals. His expertise is in helping actors and writers understand and create rich, multifaceted characters. Thus, McKee is a student of living human documents. He states, "The root of all fine character writing is self-knowledge . . . the more you penetrate the mysteries of your own humanity, the more you come to understand yourself, the more you are able to understand others."[5] McKee argues that understanding people comes from three places: facts, personal memories, and imagination.

We can use facts, personal memories, and imagination to enhance our pre-understanding. For example, when looking for facts on theological or counseling topics, I look for helpful information in print, online, and through consultations with trusted professionals. Ask yourself the following questions: What are the

5. McKee, *Story*, 72–75, 386–87.

most useful places for gaining facts about biblical topics? Which websites or software would be most helpful to you in researching these topics? Who do you go to with questions about counseling, pastoral care, or psychological issues? Are there other areas of useful information about people and care-related issues that you have yet to explore?

Personal memories and imagination are also helpful in research because they can help us relate to people on a personal level. Understanding the feelings of others is called "empathy," and it is one of a pastor's greatest skills. Pastoral counselor Carrie Doehring reminds us that "Empathy involves two simultaneous and opposite relational skills: (1) making connection with another person by experiencing what it is like to be that person, and (2) maintaining separation from the other person by being aware of one's own feelings and thoughts. Empathy is a balancing act."[6]

Empathy is vital to the hermeneutical process. It is just as important in sermon preparation as it is in pastoral counseling. In his book on preaching, Kent Edwards reminds pastors to connect with biblical narratives on a emotional level: "Look at these characters through the lens of your own life. Begin to relate on an emotional and psychological level . . . You do not want to read your own life into the biblical text. What you do want to do, however, is to truly empathize with the characters. You may not agree with them, but you must understand them."[7] Evangelicals often miss the power of emotions in texts. The empathy skills we use in our biblical interpretation can be leveraged for use in our pastoral counseling, and vice versa.

> *Empathy is vital to the hermeneutical process. It is just as important in sermon preparation as it is in pastoral counseling.*

We can use our own memories to help make these connections. If we have not had similar experiences to the person we are

6. Doehring, *Practice of Pastoral Care*, 18.

7. Edwards, *Effective First-Person Preaching*, 62–63.

counseling, we can use what Milton Terry calls a "powerful but controlled imagination" to place ourselves in similar circumstances.[8] Feeling other people's experiences as if we were them—by either remembering similar experiences from our own lives or imagining ourselves in their place—helps us with understanding, compassion, and wisdom. Ask yourself the following questions: What memories or experiences do I have that help me relate to biblical characters? What specific positive or painful experiences in my life help me to be more sensitive to hurting people? How much do I use my imagination in sermon preparation?

2. Pay Attention to Your Triggers

I was once called to visit a young couple in the emergency room of a local hospital in the middle of the night. When I arrived I found out that the couple's child had just died of Sudden Infant Death Syndrome (SIDS). SIDS occurs when an infant under the age of one, often believed to be sleeping, is found dead without any clear medical explanation, even after lengthy investigation. It is one of the worst tragedies new parents can experience. Most parents are blamed or blame themselves for not being more attentive to their sleeping child, or even for allowing too many stuffed animals in the bed. When I arrived at the hospital and heard the diagnosis, my whole body felt it. It wasn't empathy—it was something else.

> *Sometimes when we read Scripture, we are triggered. Our own pre-understanding goes into overdrive. When this happens we need to slow down, recognize that we are affected, and adjust our ministry accordingly.*

My wife and I had just had our first baby and we were still trying to get him to sleep through the night. I had left the house that night with the whimpers of our little boy in my ears. I assumed he

8. Terry, *Biblical Hermeneutics*, 23–30.

was asleep, but was he? I wasn't really present for that couple. I did my best, but I was triggered by my own life experiences.

We can also be triggered in Bible interpretation. I was once leading a small co-ed group in reading the Pastoral Epistles. One evening we read 1 Tim 2:12: "I do not permit a woman to teach or to have authority over a man; she must be silent." Before we could even talk about the context and historical situation that led the author to pen these words, a noticeable tension arose in the room. Years of discrimination against women, accusations about women being more vulnerable to false teaching, and painful experiences with previous church leaders silently bubbled to the surface. Sometimes when we read Scripture, we are triggered. Our own pre-understanding goes into overdrive. When this happens we need to slow down, recognize that we are affected, and adjust our ministry accordingly.

Recognizing the effects of our pre-understanding can be as simple noticing our body's reactions or how we are relating to others. Changes in blood pressure and heart rate are a cue that we have strong feelings or thoughts about what we are hearing. Interrupting a person while they are talking can be a sign that something personal may be going on that might be affecting our interpretation. The subtle (or obvious) presence of anger can also let us know that some part or our pre-understanding has been triggered. I recommend that pastors take a moment of silence before reading the Bible or counseling hurting people. It's an opportunity to release our cares, concerns, and mind-occupying thoughts in order to be fully available to the document in front of us.

But being triggered is not always bad. When Jesus saw the religious leaders of the day using Gentile worship spaces for overpriced temple commerce, he turned the tables over in anger (Matt 21:12–13). His knowledge of God's Word, feelings of injustice, beliefs about including non-Jews, and his non-conformist approach deeply affected his ministry. This is exactly what God wanted.

Another time, a young woman came to me expressing a desire to "be a better Christian wife." She said, "I feel like I am just so closed-off to loving my husband." She gave an example: "The other night I just didn't have time to do all I was supposed to do. I apologized and then we got into it like we always do. After he calmed down, I apologized again and said I'd try harder, but I'm just tired of trying to do everything perfectly." Her story triggered me. It reminded me of a seminar I'd been to on domestic violence. Following my gut, I asked, "What do you mean by 'then we got into it like we always do'?" Tears formed in the woman's eyes. She described her husband's yelling, insults, shaking her by the shoulders, and his arrest years ago for hitting her. My pre-understanding was triggered and it helped me to get her some much-needed protection and support.

We must be aware of when we are being triggered and make responsible decisions regarding our ministry. If you have unresolved pain about an abusive parent, providing counseling to someone who has just harmed his or her child may not be wise. If you are conflicted about your views on homosexuality, you might want to consider referring parishioners to someone with more experience in dealing with that particular issue. Like the jury selection process, we must evaluate whether our information, attitudes, ideology, and approaches to decision-making will help or hinder the people we are called to serve.

3. Remember That Learning Is a Spiral

New information and experiences cause us to reinterpret what we had previously known. We are continually learning and relearning. We all want to have the right information, attitude, worldview, and approach that will enable us to accurately understand something the first time around, but this is not a realistic expectation. Interpretation is commonly referred to as a "hermeneutical spiral." We should always see ourselves as students of written and human texts, no matter how much expertise we have. We should hold our previous understanding loosely as we pray, listen, interpret, guess, ask, clarify, and reinterpret in humility. In his book on interpreting narratives, Richard Pratt encourages an approach called the

"Authority-Dialogue Method."[9] Pratt writes that we should cultivate a cooperative relationship with texts, by which we let the text have the authority and then converse with it until we have achieved an understanding. This hermeneutical process illustrates the approach we should take in the first stages of pastoral counseling. We are there to listen and learn, not to simply reiterate or reinforce what we already believe. It is this humble and cooperative approach that makes pastors great interpreters of the Bible and empathetic pastoral counselors.

Whether we are interpreting biblical texts or living human documents, the first step of interpretation involves our pre-understanding. Recognizing that interpretation begins with the interpreter, we must know who we are, what affects our understanding, and acknowledge God's amazing work in using and changing us as we care for others. Remember:

> We cannot jump out of our own skins. We bring with us always and everywhere ourselves—that is, our presuppositions and histories, our stories. And these presuppositions enable our understanding, as well as disable it . . . The miracle is that the horizons of our presuppositions can be enlarged and transformed.[10]

Prayer

God, thank you for the amazing privilege of using us in ministering to others. We know that you are continually shaping us in our understanding of your Word and your people. Help us look within the storehouse of our lives, not as an end in itself, but as a way to be more available and useful to you in caring for hurting people. In Jesus' name, Amen.

---

9. Pratt, *He Gave Us Stories*, 23–42.

10. Green and Pasquarello, *Narrative Reading, Narrative Preaching*, 17.

Main Ideas

- We interpret life based on our previously held information, attitudes, ideology, and methodology. This is called our pre-understanding.

- Our pre-understanding can be helpful or harmful.

- We should seek to regularly inventory and enhance our storehouse of pre-understanding with facts, memories, and imagination.

- Our automatic thoughts, emotions, and simple cues from our body are ways in which we can be aware that our pre-understanding is being triggered.

- We should always be revisiting and revising our pre-understanding.

Discussion Questions

1. What did you find most significant in this chapter?

2. How could the idea of pre-understanding help you more effectively interpret Scripture or provide care to others?

3. What is an example of how facts, personal memories, and imagination have helped you relate to a passage of Scripture or care for a hurting person?

4. What is your response to the statement: "Empathy is vital to the interpretative process"?

5. Describe a time when, while studying the Bible or counseling someone, new information or experiences caused you to reinterpret what you had previously known. How does the idea that "learning is a spiral" explain how God helps us grow in our understanding of the Bible and of people?

Exercise 1: Inventorying Your Storehouse

Take some time and "inventory your storehouse" using the following questions. You may find it useful to ask people close to you to help you answer to these questions about yourself:

1. Information: On which topics do you possess the most information, knowledge, and confidence?

2. Attitudes: For which issues and topics do you have strong feelings, either positive or negative?

3. Ideology: How would you describe your theological and ideological outlook on life?

4. Methodology: How would you describe your approach to interpreting issues and solving problems?

5. Personality: How would you describe your personality? What tools, resources, or measurements have you used to assess your personality?

6. Experiences: What significant experiences, both positive and negative, have you had in your life? How do you think they have affected the way you interpret God, people, and the world?

7. Giftedness: What are your spiritual gifts, natural talents, and strengths?

Exercise 2: Enhancing Your Storehouse

We should not only inventory our storehouse, but also assess what else is needed to be more effective in interpreting written and human documents. Consider the following questions:

1. What common counseling issues do you need more information on? How could you begin to acquire this information?

2. What areas of personal bias are you aware of? How could you begin to address these?

3. What personality assessments could assist you in understanding yourself better?

4. What strong life experiences, both positive and negative, continue to powerfully influence your interpretation? Who is someone you trust to help you explore the influence of these experiences?

Exercise 3: The Storehouse of Basic Human Struggles

On a scale of one to ten, ten being the most knowledgeable, how knowledgeable are you on the following struggles commonly experienced in the course of a human life?

1. Addiction: Causes of addiction, signs of addiction versus sinful choices, Twelve Steps versus other recovery models, etc.

   1   2   3   4   5   6   7   8   9   10

2. The Grief Process: Normal responses to grief, average length of grieving time, unhelpful responses, indicators of depression, etc.

   1   2   3   4   5   6   7   8   9   10

3. Aging: Normal signs of aging versus medical conditions, how to help people through aging transitions, retirement issues, etc.

   1   2   3   4   5   6   7   8   9   10

4. Death and Dying: End of life decision-making, funeral services, personal eschatology, etc.

   1   2   3   4   5   6   7   8   9   10

5. Marital Conflict: Common issues, premarital counseling, infidelity, divorce, remarriage, etc.

   1   2   3   4   5   6   7   8   9   10

Spend time doing some basic research into items for which you scored a six or less.

Recommended Reading

Leadership beyond Reason: How Great Leaders Succeed by Harnessing the Power of Their Values, Feelings, and Intuition by John Townsend

> With years of experience in coaching and counseling spiritual leaders, Townsend helps readers explore the values, thoughts, emotions, and experiences that shape our decisions.

The Hermeneutical Spiral: A Comprehensive Introduction to Biblical Interpretation by Grant Osborne

> This is a comprehensive treatment of the hermeneutical process. Osborne has a great deal to say about the importance of pre-understanding throughout the book.

He Gave Us Stories: The Bible Student's Guide to Interpreting Old Testament Narratives by Richard Pratt

> Though aimed at interpreting Old Testament narratives, Pratt's chapter on pre-understanding discusses the influence of our sanctification, endowments, and calling.

"'Who Packed Your Bags?': Factors That Influence Our Pre-understandings" by Gary Nebeker

> Easy to understand and packed with solid research, Nebeker cites many historical and biblical examples of the impact of pre-understanding.

2

What Do You Mean?

Listening for Authorial Intention

Words, phrases, and ideas have different meanings to different people. How can we learn to listen to and understand what a text or person is trying to say rather than assuming we already know what they mean?

PASTOR DAN QUIETED ALL the questions and thoughts racing through his mind. He shifted in his seat and listened more intently to Sarah.

"The main reason I came to see you today is that my faith doesn't seem as strong as it used to be since my brother's death. My brother . . ."

She paused. Her eyes moved back and forth. "Um . . . well, what he . . ." Sarah stopped and started to say something else, but only a sigh escaped her. Her shoulders drooped. "What he did was, um . . . He took his own life. And you know what happens to people who commit suicide," she said stoically.

Sarah fell silent as a blank stare overtook her expression. It was like she was gone from the room for a moment. "But," she finally continued, sitting up straight in her chair, "I don't want to throw a spanner in the works. I've been reading the Bible more and I found a verse that says something like, 'God doesn't give you more than you can handle,' but . . ." She paused and stared off again, "I don't know." Sarah looked toward the floor, admitting, "I'm just feeling pretty overwhelmed. And, um, down."

Dan realized that Sarah was saying more with her face and her body than with her words. He asked himself, Why is she staring off like that? What could she be thinking about? Why is she having a hard time saying certain words? Why did she hang her head just now? She told me, "You know what happens to people who commit suicide," Dan thought. But what does Sarah thinks happens to someone who commits suicide? And Dan didn't understand Sarah's idioms or word choice. He asked himself, What does it mean to "throw a spanner in the works"? What does Sarah mean when she says she feels "down"? Why didn't she say, "depressed"?

How can we know what a person means? Some interpreters believe that meaning comes from the words people use. They argue that if you understand the word (written or spoken), then you understand the meaning. But this premise is problematic because words can have more than one meaning, change over time, or be used in different ways. Others believe that meaning comes from the reader or listener. They would insist, "It means what I think it means." The problem with this view is that we may come up with meanings that the author or speaker never intended.

In the real world of communication, meaning is passed from sender to receiver. Effective communication happens when the receiver properly interprets the sender's message. What something means does not inherently originate in either the words or in us, but in the person writing or speaking. What is true in conversation is true in biblical interpretation and in pastoral counseling: Meaning comes from the author's intention. This is the second step of interpretation.

What Is Authorial Intention?

As Osborne reminds us, "The goal of evangelical hermeneutics is quite simple—to discover the intention of the Author/author,"[1] that is, not only to divine the human author's intentions, but those of God, who inspires the text. Understanding intent is of paramount importance. In legal cases, intentions can be the difference between first-degree murder and involuntary manslaughter. In medicine, administering a dose of morphine (a painkiller that can fatally slow the heart) can constitute either physician-assisted suicide or palliative end-of-life care, depending on intent. In conversation, it can be the difference between an insult and a friendly joke. Intention comes from the inner thoughts and knowledge in a person's heart (Heb 4:12). Putting an author's intentions before our own is at the heart of evangelical hermeneutics. This requires a faithful commitment on the part of the interpreter.

> *Putting an author's intentions before our own is at the heart of evangelical hermeneutics. This requires a faithful commitment on the part of the interpreter.*

Let us consider Kevin Vanhoozer's claim that pastors must possess four "interpretive virtues" that will ensure a commitment to authorial intent: honesty, openness, attentiveness, and obedience.[2]

1. Am I Honest with Myself?

We must be honest about how easy it is for our ideas and intentions to become more important than the author's. In regards to biblical interpretation: Can I admit that I am biased towards certain interpretations, views, and genres? Will I stop myself in my sermon preparation when I sense that time, agendas, or personal

1. Osborne, *Hermeneutical Spiral*, 24.
2. Vanhoozer, *Is There a Meaning?* 377.

preferences are steering me away from the author's intention? With regard to pastoral counseling: Can I admit that I am biased toward or against certain people, problems, and solutions? Will I reevaluate my heart when I find myself counseling people in a way that is more about me than them?

2. Am I Open to the Ideas of Others?

We must ask if we are genuinely interested in the thoughts and feelings of others. Regarding biblical interpretation: Am I willing to seriously consider theological views that differ from my own? Am I open to entertaining an alternate view of a passage of Scripture? In regards to pastoral counseling: Am I willing to listen carefully to someone, even when I completely disagree with what they are saying? Am I open to trying to understand their point of view even though I may believe it to be wrong?

3. Am I Attentive to the Needs of Others?

We must not be self-absorbed in our ministry. We must ask ourselves in biblical interpretation: Am I aware of what the author is trying to argue, or do I just want to use the text to support my own message? Do I see the linguistic, cultural, and historical elements of the passage, or am I singularly focused on how I want to understand the text? In regards to pastoral counseling: Am I aware of the counselee's goals and desires, or am I moving them toward my own agenda? Do I see the spiritual, emotional, physical, and relational elements of this person's struggle, or am I too focused on one specific area?

4. Am I Able to Follow Others' Leading?

This doesn't necessarily mean doing what others say; we must honor what is said in context. With regard to biblical interpretation: Am I reading the genre according the conventions of the genre? Am I following the author's flow of thought and rhetorical purpose? Am I arriving at the conclusion the author intends? In regards to pastoral counseling: Am I tracking with the mood and purpose of the counselee's sharing? Am I following the person's train of thought?

In the midst of the busy demands of the pastoral office, these interpretive virtues can keep us focused on the author's intended meaning, whether that author is the writer of a biblical text or hurting person seeking counseling.

Reducing Barriers to Interpretation

There are many obstacles to listening. Effective listening is about doing whatever it takes to allow the author's meaning to be sovereign, which includes consciously reducing any internal and external barriers that might prevent us from listening for the author's intent.

Internal barriers to listening include our need to fix, our sense of time, pride, and preoccupation with other matters. The Bible reminds us, "Everyone should be quick to listen, slow to speak and slow to become angry" (Jas 1:19). Listening involves slowing down and not assuming we understand everything we are reading or hearing. Sometimes our lack of time or lack of humility will lead us to jump to conclusions. Answering with limited information is a characteristic of fools (Prov 18:11). Pastors should be known for their desire to learn through active listening (Prov 21:11).

> *Listening is not about simply hearing words, but being committed to understanding the author's meaning.*

Listening is not about simply hearing words, but being committed to understanding the author's meaning. It is the difference between hearing and understanding. Jesus used parables and riddles that guided people to search for his intended meaning. His words were heard by many, but his teaching required those seeking understanding to do more internal work (Mark 4:11–12). Jesus encouraged people to ask him questions, and he asked questions in return. Asking questions is a primary way to clarify meaning and bring down internal barriers.

External barriers to listening include the physical environment. In communication theory, anything that interferes with the receiver's ability to hear and understand the sender is called "noise." Neh 8:1–3 records Ezra gathering the Israelites together to hear the reading of the Law. He created the best environment for the people to hear God's Word, building a special pulpit so everyone could hear the Law directly. This allowed the people to listen to the author for themselves. Whether reading a written or human document, how a room is arranged, sound quality, privacy, and comfort level all work to minimize physical distractions in hopes of reducing external barriers that might hinder understanding the author's intent.

Language and Mood

Word usage is important in listening for intention. Unfortunately, the meaning of words is not as simple as it may appear because "language is fraught with possible ambiguity, misinterpretation, and unthinking assumptions."[3] Words have what is called a semantic range. Consider Paul's use of the words σομα (*soma*) and σαρξ (*sarx*) in Rom 7:14–25. Both words can be translated as "flesh" and both are used to refer to the physical body created by God for ministry in this life, but σαρξ is also used several times to refer to humankind's earthly, sinful nature apart from divine influence. How this word is used dramatically affects its meaning.[4] Another example of how a word can carry more than one meaning is Κυριος (*kyrios*) which is translated as "Lord." Κυριος can communicate respect to a person in a superior position or take on cosmic theological significance when applied to Jesus Christ. Thus, understanding an author's words demands a consideration

3. Payne, *Narrative Therapy*, 8.

4. See Moo, "'Flesh' in Romans," 365–79.

of context, tense, semantic fallacies, as well as a wide range of other exegetical tools.

Discerning the difference between literal and non-literal language is also helpful in determining authorial intent. Jesus often used non-literal and figurative language, including anthropomorphisms, euphemisms, metaphors, hyperbole, and metonymy. When it comes to listening for an author's intention, "figures of speech demand active reading on the interpreter's part. Such reading is no spectator sport for the hermeneutically lazy or indifferent exegete."[5]

Non-literal language is often essential to understanding an author's mood. Feelings are often communicated with non-literal language. Haddon Robinson suggests using painful experiences from our own lives to better understand the mood of the author. This is especially important when interpreting literary forms that rely heavily on mood, such as poetry, because mood is often implicit within the genre. So it is that pastors must learn to interpret not only the language, but also the mood of texts. For many of us, this means increasing our ability to recognize and understand feelings. This capability is commonly referred to as "emotional intelligence." As Robinson advises us, "You can find it helpful . . . when you are wrestling with a passage of Scripture, the Psalms, or something else, to ask not only, what is the author saying, but what is the writer wanting us to feel?"[6]

> When body language is described in Scripture, we should pay careful attention because "nonverbals are powerful and they have meaning."

Non-verbal communication is also important in biblical interpretation. Most communication happens through people's actions. Facial expressions, body posture, eye contact, tone of voice, and a wide variety of other forms of non-verbal communication carry keys to understanding author's intention. When body

5. Köstenberger and Patterson, *Invitation to Biblical Interpretation*, 674.

6. Robinson et al., "Preach through Painful Experiences," http://www.gordonconwell.edu/resources/Archives.cfm.

language is described in Scripture, we should pay careful attention because "nonverbals are powerful and they have meaning."[7] The Apostle Paul's farewell address to the Ephesian elders sounds like a picture of stately theological resolve, but the consideration that the narrative ends with a description of an incredibly emotional time of weeping, grief, and intimacy dictates our interpretation of the mood of the text (Acts 20:13–38).

Deep Structure, Subtext, and Intertextuality

The meaning of an author's text is not always clearly seen on the surface. People think, feel, and act based on a set of core beliefs. Their theology is rarely articulated overtly and is often formed over time by education and experiences. What lies beneath or behind the words of the author involves studying what is called deep structure, subtext, and intertextuality.

Deep structure refers to the theological beliefs encoded or embedded into what a person is saying. Grant Osborne illustrates deep structure by looking for what he calls "kernel sentences."[8] In Eph 2:8–9, Paul writes, "For it is by grace you have been saved, through faith—and this is not from yourselves, it is the gift of God—not by works, so that no one can boast." Studying the structural syntax of this verse leads us to seven simple theological truths: (1) God showed you grace, (2) God saved you, (3) you believed, (4) you did not save yourselves, (5) God gave you salvation, (6) you did not work for it, and (7) this is done so that no man can boast.[9] Paul does not explicitly or propositionally state these seven theological truths, but they are embedded in what he does say, helping us to better understand the author's message.

Deep structure can be found in the words of those we counsel. For example, after several long days away from home, a husband decides to join his friends for a third night of watching sports at a local bar. His wife responds, "You're going there again?" There is

7. Navarro, *Every Body Is Saying*, 5.

8. Osborne, *Hermentical Spiral*, 115.

9. Ibid.

more to her question than what he might hear on the surface. Her question contains several possible embedded beliefs and feelings: (1) I don't want you to go there tonight, (2) you are not spending enough time at home, (3) I miss you, or (4) I am jealous of your ability to go do whatever you want. Deep structure is what we listen for to discover the core beliefs lying within and beneath what a person is saying.

Subtext refers to "the life under the surface—thoughts and feelings both known and unknown, hidden by the author . . . Text and subtext is made up of what is said, what is unsaid and what is unsayable."[10] Literary theorists and dramatists look for subtext to reveal the motivations behind what people ask, say, and do. It is the story behind the words. When Jesus was teaching his followers about loving one's neighbors, one man asked: "Who is my neighbor?" On the surface, this seems like a legitimate question aimed at understanding how to apply God's Word. But Luke reveals the motive behind the question, saying, "But he

> *Deep structure reveals embedded beliefs, while subtext reveals embedded motivations.*

wanted to justify himself, so he asked Jesus, 'and who is my neighbor?'" (Luke 10:29). Deep structure reveals embedded beliefs, while subtext reveals embedded motivations.

One of my favorite examples of subtext is from the movie *Toy Story*. The movie is told from the perspective of Woody, a cowboy toy belonging to a boy named Andy. Being Andy's favorite toy is what Woody's life is all about. During a musical montage we see how much Woody enjoys being loved, wanted, and played with by Andy. Tragedy strikes when Andy gets a brand-new toy for his birthday—Buzz Lightyear, a super-cool astronaut action-figure boasting lights, buttons, and space lingo that gadget-less Woody just can't compete with. Like me, you may be able to relate to being an older model in the presence of newer, flashier toys. Thrilled with his birthday surprise, Andy excitedly pushes Woody off the

10. McKee, *Story*, 252.

prized spot on the bed to give Buzz pride of place. Woody's expression remains the same, a painted-on smile, but the filmmakers trust that we know what lies beneath that perpetual grin—disappointment, rejection, and jealousy. It isn't shown, but we know the heartbreak Woody feels. That is subtext.

Intertextuality refers to when an author directly or indirectly references another source, and in doing so, draws upon the borrowed text's ideas, themes, or mood to make his or her point. When Jesus refers to a "vine" or "fertile garden" (John 15:1–11), he may want his listeners to consider how these metaphors are used in reference to Israel in the Hebrew Scriptures (Isa 5:1–2). In Phil 1:18–20, when Paul defends his ministry against his accusers, he uses a semantic structure similar to Job 13:16. Paul may have wanted his readers to see a connection between himself and Job, "the righteous sufferer."[11] So it is that a quote or reference to another source can help us better understand an author's intent.

Authorial Intention in Pastoral Counseling

1. Practice Intentional Listening

Great pastors do not simply listen long enough to correct an error, clarify doctrine, or answer a direct question. They practice "intentional listening." Pastors pay attention to words, feelings, and non-verbal communication in order to understand the people who come to them for help because "meanings are in people, not in words."[12] Intentional listening involves active listening skills like repeating, rephrasing, and asking open-ended questions.

I once met with a man in his mid-thirties who told me, "I'm really struggling. I just want to be able to get into the Word." I asked him, "You want to 'get into the Word.' What do you mean by that?" He replied, "You know, really get into the Bible." I asked, "What would that look like?" He responded, "I hear about all these

11. Fee, *Paul's Letter to the Philippians*, 130–38.
12. Wakefield, *Between the Words*, 123.

people who have, like, an hour-long prayer and Bible reading time every day, and I don't have that! I want that!" By repeating and rephrasing what was confided and asking clarifying questions, I was finally able to understand his meaning. I realized that "getting into the Word" meant something very specific to this man. It was a code for a very particular experience he had heard about. If I had assumed the meaning of "getting into the Word," I might have dispensed bad advice and would not have been able to conduct the conversation that followed, during which we explored where the man's desire for such a powerful spiritual experience was coming from. Intentional listening is about slowing down, asking questions, and looking to understand the person behind the words. As pastors, our hermeneutical methods teach us to patiently and thoughtfully explore authors' meanings.

Another way to practice intentional listening is to allow counselees the space to fully share their thoughts and feelings. In hermeneutics, we refer to this practice as "reading thought units." As when interpreting a text, we need to listen long enough to discover the "flow of thought" or the "big picture" of a person's story. This is especially important because most people need time to help make the connections between what they are saying, thinking, and

> *As when interpreting a text, we need to listen long enough to discover the "flow of thought" or the "big picture" of a person's story.*

feeling. In seminary, I was encouraged to read entire books of the Bible in one sitting to ensure I got the big picture of the author's thoughts. We certainly do not have the time or patience to hear a person's entire life story, but we need to allow enough time to locate the controlling idea of a person's thoughts. We'll explore this notion further in chapter 4.

Intentional listening takes work. As Wayne Mack explains, "Pastors, in particular, may find it difficult to listen to counselees. Gifted in teaching and accustomed to speaking from the pulpit, a pastor tends to take a one-sided approach in counseling."[13] We should see intentional listening as the research phase of our pastoral counseling. More like exegesis than preaching, this step is about listening, thinking, and asking questions of the text, not talking. When we do talk, it should be to make sure that what we have heard is what the author intended. Our goal should be to grasp a person's thoughts and feelings and be able to repeat these back to them in our own words to check our understanding. The late Henri Nouwen referred to this as the pastoral skill of "articulation" and believed it was essential to spiritual leadership in the future.[14] In practicing these skills we imitate God, who is described in Scripture as one who listens and understands (Gen 21:17–18; Ps 116:1–2; John 11:41–42).

2. Pay Attention to Non-Verbal and Non-Literal Communication

When people come to counseling, much of their communication is non-verbal: "Few people fully grasp the importance of nonverbal communication, despite the fact that is common knowledge among communication researchers that approximately 60 to 65 percent of our meaning is expressed nonverbally."[15] Former FBI agent Joe Navarro, in his book, *What Every Body Is Saying*, describes seven different non-verbal cues in order to ascertain meaning: facial expressions, physical movements (kinesics), body distance (proxemics), touching (haptics), vocal tone, timbre, and volume.[16] In caring for hurting people, we should ask ourselves: What is this person saying with their body language? What does their voice tell me about their words and thoughts? In what ways does their body match what they are saying? In what ways are they different?

13. Mack, "Taking Counselee Inventory," 211.
14. Nouwen, *Wounded Healer*, 37–38.
15. Wakefield, *Between the Words*, 49.
16. Navarro, *Every Body is Saying*, xi–xiv.

We listen for meaning with our eyes as well as our ears. For example, one man came to counseling with questions about time management. He talked about how much his work meant to him, the arrival of a new granddaughter, and his growing involvement in a ministry at the church. He said he loved and felt called to all these commitments. After a few minutes, he breathed a great sigh, his shoulders sagged, and his eyes froze as if fixed on something invisible. I waited for a few seconds before asking, "What just happened there—with your body and your eyes?" He thought it over and replied, "I was feeling like a juggler who can't keep things in the air. I was thinking, 'God please take something away from me.'" Non-verbal communication is filled with meaning.

Non-literal speech is another way to explore meaning. Both Scripture and people should not always be taken literally. Much depends on the author's intention. Non-literal language is a powerful form of communication because figurative speech is one of the most effective ways to communicate emotions. Therefore, we should pay careful attention to the metaphors, figures of speech, and idioms people use. Consider the following examples of non-literal language and their meanings:

Expression	Non-Literal Form	Meaning/Feeling
The honeymoon was like heaven.	Simile (comparing two things with like or as)	Best imaginable
You never help me with the children!	Hyperbole (overstatement or exaggeration for effect)	Frustration, desperation, anger
This girl wanted to hook up with me last night after work.	Euphemism (harmless word used to replace an offensive one)	Have a sexual encounter
Yeah, right. If I just pray, things will change.	Sarcasm (sharp, bitter comment reflecting the opposite of what is said)	Futility about prayer, God, or hopelessness
Throw a spanner in the works.	Idiom (special phrase with a figurative meaning)	British expression for "wrench" that refers to causing trouble or stopping something from succeeding

When someone uses non-literal language, consider asking the speaker to explain their meaning further. This can unlock a discussion about emotions and intentions. Consider someone saying, "I just want to die." Does this person have a plan in place to commit suicide, or is this an intentional exaggeration (hyperbole) intended to make a point? In this situation, discerning the difference between literal and non-literal language could have dramatic consequences.

3. Listen Beneath the Surface

When people face a crisis, "their first attempts at answers come out of their embedded theology, out of the theological presuppositions that shape their lives and practices."[17] Their embedded theology may not be biblical, coherent, or even consistent, but it is the place from which people interpret their lives. Another woman came to me for counseling after acting out in fit of rage against her husband. During the discussion, she disclosed that she had been sexually abused as a child by an elderly neighbor. She saw a connection between her past abuse and her current feelings, but she felt very confused. She told me, "I've forgiven my abuser like I should. So why am I still mad?" In her statement I heard what sounded like some core beliefs. I wrote down the following:

Statement Embedded	Theology/Core Belief
I've forgiven my abuser.	I have done what I needed to do to forgive.
As I should.	I am required to forgive (ready or not?)
Why am I still mad?	When you forgive, you will feel better.

This woman's question belied core beliefs about forgiveness, healing, and recovery. She had never really thought about them before, but they were there. Painful experiences in her back-story and triggers in her present life were challenging her beliefs. As pastors, we can use our hermeneutical training in deep structure and

17. Doehring, *Practice of Pastoral Care*, 112.

subtext to help people discover and examine the core beliefs that drive their behavior.

We must also listen for intertextuality. People quote, cite, and make allusive references to a variety of sources to help explain themselves. These sources may come from the Bible, movies, famous quotes, song lyrics, or other stories they have come across. Pop-culture references are increasingly common today. Pastors need to develop a "media midrash" in order to help make sense of counselees' references.[18] Of course, the most effective way to explore intertextuality is by asking the author what he or she means by the reference. In one pastoral counseling session, a woman said that she had recently quit her job and broken up with her boyfriend. She asked me, "Did you see *Eat Pray Love?*" I had not. She mentioned that she'd really enjoyed it and went on to ask me a question about prayer. Instead of answering her question, I asked, "What was so great about that movie?" She told me about the main character's courage to start her life over in a radical way. This movie reference led us to a discussion about the difference between the courage to start over and running away from life's challenges.

Every person operates from a set of beliefs about God, self, and the world. These beliefs are rarely verbalized, but they nevertheless shape a person's thoughts, feelings, reasoning, and actions. Variously referred to as silent assumptions, core beliefs, or embedded theology, these beliefs are all part of the counselee's pre-understanding. Just as we need to inventory and assess our own pre-understanding, we must help others dig beneath the surface of conversation to explore their pre-understanding. As we listen, we can begin to ask ourselves: What unspoken beliefs appear to shape this person's life? Based on what this person is saying, what does he or she appear to believe about God, self, people, and the world? What references does this person make, and how can these references help me better understand his or her thoughts, feelings, and actions?

18. Cusick, "Clown," 17.

Whether we are interpreting biblical texts or living human documents, the second step of interpretation involves determining authorial intent. We listen to what is said, what goes unsaid, how it is said, and what lurks beneath the words to look for what a person *really* means—not what we want them to mean. In the context of pastoral care and counseling, we approach a person much like a biblical text. Like standing before a sacred painting or sculpture, we ask the Holy Spirit to slow us down and help us remain open. As C. S. Lewis said: "The first demand any work of art makes upon us is surrender. Look. Listen. Receive."[19]

Prayer

God, thank you for listening and understanding us. Our thoughts, feelings, and what we really mean is deep within us, but you draw these things out. Slow us down as we minister to others. Help us to imitate you by listening, asking thoughtful questions, and paying attention to not only what we hear, but also what we see. In Jesus' name, Amen.

Main Ideas

- The goal of evangelical hermeneutics is to discover the original author's meaning.

- The interpretive virtues of honesty, openness, attentiveness, and obedience will help us in our search for an author's meaning.

- Listening for what a person means includes paying attention to language, mood, and to non-literal and non-verbal communication.

19. Quoted in Vanhoozer, *Is There a Meaning?* 139.

- People think, feel, and act based on a set of core beliefs. This embedded theology is rarely articulated and is formed by a person's experiences.

Discussion Questions

1. What concepts in this chapter did you find most significant?

2. Which of the four interpretive virtues do you believe you practice most when reading Scripture? When counseling people?

3. Why is the skill of "articulation" so important for pastors?

4. Many pastors think and relate cognitively, while many people seeking counseling need to relate emotionally. Why is emotional expression and emotional intelligence under-emphasized in some seminaries and churches, and what can we do to enhance our own?

5. In what ways do deep structure, subtext, and intertextuality help you in your interpretation of Scripture? In your interpretation of people?

Exercise 1: Barriers to Listening

Careful listening is an essential discipline in understanding Scripture as well as people. We need to understand our own barriers and work to compensate for them during interpretation. Look over the following common barriers to listening and indicate which occur most often for you and under what specific circumstances:

1. I am uninterested in what is being said.

2. I am busy thinking of what to say.

3. I am distracted/too concerned by my own issues.

4. I am falsely convinced that I understand what's been said.

5. I am uncomfortable with silence.

6. I am over-confident of my ability to help.

7. I have overly simplistic views about spiritual, emotional, and psychological issues.

On a scale of one to ten, with ten being a great listener, what score would you give yourself? What number would your spouse, children, or congregants for you?

Exercise 2: Assessing Your Emotional Intelligence

Emotions are like colors; there are many shades and hues. It is helpful to have a robust emotional vocabulary capable of expressing these many shades of difference. Write five alternate words for the following emotions:

1. Sad:

2. Happy:

3. Angry:

4. Lonely:

5. Confused:

Recommended Reading

Between the Words: The Art of Perceptive Listening by Norm Wakefield

An easy to understand biblical resource on active listening skills for Christians.

What Every Body Is Saying: An Ex-FBI Agent's Guide to Speed-Reading People by Joe Navarro

As a former FBI counterintelligence agent, Navarro offers simple techniques for interpreting people's body language.

Let the Reader Understand: A Guide to Interpreting and Applying the Bible by Dan McCartney and Charles Clayton

> The authors offer a useful genenral overview of hermeneutics with an outstanding chapter on understanding non-literal language, including figures of speech found in the Bible.

Is There Meaning in This Text? The Bible, the Reader, and the Morality of Literary Knowledge by Kevin J. Vanhoozer

> A thorough treatment of the subject of hermeneutics with great attention to the interpretive virtues needed to honor authorial intention.

"Don't Turn Exegesis into an Autopsy" by Scott M. Gibson

> In this podcast, Gordon-Conwell Theological Seminary's Dr. Scott M. Gibson discusses the necessity of understanding emotions in exegesis and the dangers of being too rational and scientific in our treatment of the Scriptures.

3

Can I Get Some Background?

History, Culture, and Circumstantial Context

Culture, history, and other background information are sometimes the key to interpretation. How can we look behind what is written or said to understand the important issues that lie beneath the surface?

PASTOR DAN WAITED QUIETLY as Sarah shared her story. He felt she needed space to be in that moment. As Sarah haltingly admitted that she had been feeling down, Dan thought about a few questions he could ask, but then Sarah looked up and continued more confidently.

"I've been thinking about my mom a lot lately," she said. "We're from the South. And my mom . . . well, she was pretty difficult." She hesitated. "In fact, she ended up at Dix Hill. We went to visit her one time. It was a pretty horrible place."

Pastor Dan saw Sarah pick up on the curiosity that crossed his face. "Dix Hill is a . . . It's the kind of place you send people when they're not functioning well." Sarah shrugged, "She was just crazy. And that was really tough on us—I never want to be like my mom." She sat up with a slight smile. "What I want to be like that woman in Proverbs 31," she said, "so confident and strong."

Dan wondered why Sarah had been thinking about her mom. He asked himself, What do her Southern roots have to do with this, or more importantly, her mother? Is Dix Hill a psychiatric facility? What was her mom's diagnosis? Why did Sarah have such a hard time talking about it? Dan was grateful that Sarah was able to reach that moment of honesty. He found it very revealing that she never wanted to be like her mom. He wondered, What must it have been like growing up in such a home? How had Sarah's mother shaped her views of God, herself, and the world? Where was her father? How are all these different parts of Sarah's past coming together now, with the death of her brother?

Interpretation is similar to putting together a puzzle without the box. We are not always sure which pieces are needed in order to see the big picture. These puzzle pieces come in a variety of shapes and sizes—present or past, big or small, they all are important to understanding the whole story. This is what we call context. It is the third step of interpretation.

What Is Context?

History, culture, and circumstances can all shape an author's meaning. Consider the following example: A woman was waiting at a bus stop for her ride home. When the bus arrived she found an available seat and made herself comfortable. As the bus continued from stop to stop, the seats began to fill up. At the next stop, the driver asked her to move to another seat. She refuses. Busses often get overcrowded, and passengers stake claims to seats all the time. How does context change our interpretation of this story? The year was 1955 and the place was Montgomery, Alabama. Rosa Parks, an African American woman, was told up to move to the back of the bus to make room for a white man. She may not have intended to spark the bus boycotts and larger civil rights movement that swept the Jim Crow South, but her actions, together with a local civil rights group led by a young Baptist minister named Martin Luther King Jr., led to changes that ended segregation throughout the United States.

Understanding context helps us more fully grasp the meaning of words and feelings. Context can turn spare facts into vibrant, living stories. In sermon preparation, contextual understanding can "turn a sermon from a two-dimensional study to a three-dimensional cinematic event."[1] In exploring context, we become a kind of Indiana Jones, excavating information from archeology, history, anthropology, sociology, and other disciplines in order to understand the bigger picture of the text's meaning. In general, when looking at context, we draw from three major areas:

1. Historical Context

What past experiences or events will help me better understand the text? How essential is the past or present setting to the meaning of the text? In regards to biblical interpretation: Where does this text fall in God's progressive revelation? What is its historical-redemptive context? What have these biblical characters gone through already, and how does this shape their actions? With regard to pastoral counseling: What events and have shaped who this person is today? How have they experienced God in their past, and how does this effect their views today? Where is this person on their life journey (i.e., stages of development)?

2. Cultural Context

How do regional, geographic, and socio-economic factors, along with ethical values and cultural norms, play into understanding the meaning of this text? Does this text contain traditions and mores that are different than my own? Regarding biblical interpretation: Does the biblical character's ethnicity or nationality help me understand their words and actions? What unique religious practices does this person or group possess? How does this person's culture understand issues like age, gender, education, politics, slavery, body image, gender, or power? In regards to pastoral counseling:

1. Osborne, *Hermeneutical Spiral*, 158.

What is the ethnic background of the person I am counseling, and how does that relate to the struggle they are facing? In what ways might this person's traditions and outlook be different than my own?

3. Circumstantial Context

What is the immediate setting from which (or to which) the author is writing? What situation is motivating the author to speak and act? What is this author trying to accomplish or persuade us to believe? With regard to biblical interpretation: What is the rhetorical purpose of the text, genre, or book? What is the specific situation the author is facing? What is the author trying to do in that situation (change it, maintain it, endure it)? In regards to pastoral counseling: What is the presenting problem of the counselee? Why has this person come for counseling? What is this person facing, and what are they wanting of God in this situation?

We cannot venture too far from the grand story of Scripture without seeing the importance of historical context. The Bible is a historical book. Scripture describes God in reference to the historical figures of "Abraham, Isaac and Jacob" (Exod 3:6; Matt 22:32; Acts 3:13). When the Israelites celebrated the great feasts (Lev 23) or worshiped in praises and laments (Pss 44, 78:1–4), their understanding of God and of each other was grounded in their understanding of history. Biblical stories also assume the reader is aware of cultural issues. In the narrative of the woman at the well in John 4, Jesus ministers to a Samaritan woman of questionable reputation. A basic understanding of first-century religion, ethnicity, gender, and politics allows us to see the revolutionary nature of Jesus' ministry as well as his pastoral skill in isolating spiritual issues from socio-political and religious debates. The New Testament letters perhaps best exemplify the importance of circumstantial context. Paul wrote to specific situations believers were facing (1 Cor 5:1, 8:1, 11:8). These three kinds of context are extremely important in interpretation because without them "the interpreter may inadvertently impose an alien point of view onto the text, distorting its meaning."[2]

Understanding Distance

The difference between our own values, norms, and traditions, and those of the author is called "distance." Distance creates the potential for misunderstanding and misinterpretation: "A good Bible student must be able to identify the differences between the world of the text and the world of the audience and then build a bridge between these two worlds so that the message heard by its original audience is heard by the new audience with all the same authority and implications."[3] In Neh 8, Ezra realized that some of the Israelites did not understand Hebrew. This was linguistic distance. To address this difference, he assigned translators throughout the crowd who could explain the Scripture as it was being read. In Acts 8, the Ethiopian eunuch had educational, cultural, and spiritual distance from the text of Isaiah. Philip bridged the distance by patiently explaining the passage, which resulted in the eunuch's conversion and baptism. In Luke 24, the disciples experienced what could be considered existential or psychological distance. Traumatized and confused by the crucifixion, they were unable to recognize the risen Christ. Only after a thorough review of the Hebrew prophecies and a familiar communion meal was the distance bridged such that they were able believe in his resurrection.

On a practical level, much of the distance between biblical texts and our own understanding has to do with differences in basic values. The fields of missiology and intercultural studies have provided much guidance in this area. In their book, *Ministering Cross Culturally: An Incarnational Model for Personal Relationships*, Sherwood Lingenfelter and Marvin Mayers suggest six categories for discovering what has been called "the silent language of culture."[4]

2. Ferguson, *Biblical Hermenuetics*, 71.

3. Ralston, "Showing the Relevance," 295.

4. Lingenfelter and Mayers, *Ministering Cross-Culturally*, 27.

1. Time versus Event Orientation	Time Orientation *Values*: Punctuality, scheduling, and time limits	Event Orientation *Values*: People involved, events, and present experience
2. Task versus Person Orientation	Task Orientation *Values*: Actions and developing relationships based on goal achievement	Person Orientation *Values*: Relationships and finding satisfaction in group experiences
3. Dichotomistic versus Holistic Orientation	Dichotomistic Orientation *Values*: Making judgments based on clearly communicated systems of right and wrong	Holistic Orientation *Values*: Open-ended discussion including a wide range of opinions and interactions in decision-making
4. Status versus Achievement Orientation	Status Orientation *Values*: Identity in socially-fixed factors like birth and rank	Achievement Orientation *Values*: Identity in personal achievements and accomplishments
5. Crisis versus Non-crisis Orientation	Crisis Orientation *Values*: Anticipating problems, planning ahead, seeking expert advice	Non-crisis Orientation *Values*: Downplaying crisis, delaying decisions, and distrusting expert advice
6. Concealment of Vulnerability versus Willingness to Expose Vulnerability	Concealment of Vulnerability *Values*: Self-image, hiding weaknesses, and being uncomfortable with criticism	Willingness to Expose Vulnerability *Values*: Admitting shortcomings, self-image based on authenticity, and being open to criticism

Misreadings and misinterpretations come when our values differ from those we are studying. Recognizing our differences and bridging the distance with regard to basic values is part of honoring historical, cultural, and circumstantial context.[5]

---

5. Ricoeur, Gadamer, Geertz, and others refer to the process of recognizing and compensating for differences to ensure proper interpretation as "distanciation." See Carson, *Exegetical Fallacies*.

Patterns, Conventions, Synoptical Reading, and Narrative Coding

If I were to say, "A priest, a rabbi, and a minister walk into a bar," a smile might come to your face because you're expecting something funny. Why? It is because the structure of my sentence caused you to recognize a literary pattern—a joke. Literary critics call this "synoptical reading" or "narrative coding." It is the underlying structure that helps guide us in our reading and interpretation. As Robert Scholes explains, "Reading is a largely unconscious activity. We can only read a story if we have read enough other stories to understand the basic elements of narrative coding . . . the ideal reader shares the author's codes and is able to process the text without confusion or delay."[6] That is, we can read and understand more quickly and easily when we can identify a pattern to what is being said.

Thus, understanding context involves recognizing structures, patterns, and conventions that authors employ to assist readers in understanding their meaning. Patterns are found in literature in the form of genre, archetypes, and tropes, but patterns can also be found in cultures and people. In his book on reading and interpreting cultural trends, Kevin Vanhoozer writes that understanding culture is "a matter of discerning patterns, especially as these involve the relation between embedded parts and their larger meaningful whole."[7] When we say that the Jewish culture of the first century was primarily patriarchal in its spiritual leadership, had strong distinctions between male and female interaction, and generally resisted Roman political authority, we are not stereotyping or un-

> *Patterns are found in literature in the form of genre, archetypes, and tropes, but patterns can also be found in cultures and people.*

6. Scholes, *Textual Power*, 21–22, quoted in Long, *Preaching and the Literary Forms*, 18.

7. Vanhoozer et al., *Everyday Theology*, 22.

fairly profiling a group of people. We are recognizing patterns. Discerning cultural patterns give us a head start in the interpretive process.

Patterns can also be found in human personality. We can see the unique communication style of biblical writers: John wrote his Gospel in the third person, Mark wrote his Gospel with a sense of spiritual urgency, and Paul borrowed Roman imperial cult metaphors when discussing the Second Coming of Christ. Debates about the author of Hebrews often revolve around looking for patterns within the book that correspond with the writing patterns of other writers. By recognizing patterns in an author's writing style, we can know some of what to expect from their writing.

Incarnational Ministry

By attending to historical, cultural, and circumstantial context, we are reinforcing our understanding of the incarnation. God did not stand apart from or reject the world; rather, God entered fully into it. In Jesus Christ, God lived, taught, healed, and redeemed people through full immersion into human history, culture, and people's immediate circumstances. For centuries, missionaries have followed God's example of "incarnational ministry" by immersing themselves in new cultures, customs, and languages to find ways to understand people and introduce them to the gospel. Pastoral counseling follows the same incarnational model. We seek to understand people's unique historical, cultural, and circumstantial context in order to discover how God is already at work in their world. Only then can we find ways to bridge the distance between their world and the world of the gospel in contextualized ways.

Context in Pastoral Counseling

1. Explore the Person's History, Culture, and Circumstances

As Kollar explains, "In counseling, the context is often difficult to discern. To apply truth to an individual case accurately, the counselor must be fully aware of all the details of the situation."[8] Context can protect us from giving premature advice, overly simplistic answers, and from having to retract guidance when a new piece of information adds another layer to a person's presenting problem. A simple way to explore context is by making use of an inventory or checklist before someone comes in for counseling. This can include physical, emotional, and behavioral issues, as well as a person's basic beliefs, personal history, and resources.[9]

Many pastors feel that a pre-counseling inventory works against the informal nature of pastoral counseling; therefore, a more organic or narrative approach may be better. Questions can be asked at the beginning of and throughout the counseling session in order to explore context. Below is a list of suggested questions along with the kind of contexts these questions are designed to explore:

What brings you here today?	Circumstantial
When did this situation or feeling begin?	Circumstantial Historical
Have you ever gone through this before? If so, what did you do last time?	Historical
What have you been doing about this up until this point?	Historical
What support or advice, if any, have you been given about this? By whom (friends, pastors, counselors, etc.)?	Historical Cultural
What have you been telling yourself about what is going on?	Historical Cultural
What are you hoping to get out of our time together today?	Circumstantial

A person's history can reveal important information about their past, including their childhood. Sometimes details from the past can provide insight into current struggles. Not every

8. Kollar, *Solution-Focused Pastoral Counseling*, 41.

9. Mack, "Taking Counselee Inventory," 210–30.

present-day challenge is rooted in childhood issues, but people are formed over time through their upbringing, self-talk, relationships, and education. Asking about a person's background can sometimes reveal important clues about present-day behavior.

In collecting background information, sometimes we hear things that don't make sense to us. This is a clue that there may be cultural differences that need to be understood. For example, in one of my seminary classes, a Korean pastor told the story of a couple who visited his church. The wife was a Korean woman in her fifties and her husband was Caucasian. As this couple made their way to an open seat, the pastor made sure to welcome them in a very public way. Sharing the story, the pastor told us, "I wanted to make sure everyone saw me accept them." I nodded in approval, but saw the other Korean students nodding much more vigorously. I felt like I was missing something, so I asked, "Why did you want to make sure everyone saw you accept them?" He replied, "Our churches are very conservative and have high moral expectations. A woman of that age would have probably met her husband while he was a soldier. Some people think there are only certain places that a young Korean girl would meet a soldier." With his characteristic reserve, he did not elaborate further. Instead he said, "I wanted all of the other women in the church to see that we should not be judging or thinking ill of this woman. If I, as the pastor, can accept her and her husband, then they should too." This pastor ministered effectively to that new couple because he was appropriately aware of the importance of cultural context. When I got home, I told my wife the first part of the story. She started nodding just like the Korean students had. My wife is Vietnamese, so she understood the contextual issue and shared a similar story about her own cultural background.

We should pay attention to the small clues that remind us to think about cultural context. These can include accents, figures of speech, idioms, a different flow of logic, or something as simple as an unexpected reaction in conversation. A humorous story from a friend of mine illustrates this point. My friend Marcus bought a scooter, knowing that scooters are an easy way to get around in

Southern California beach communities. Marcus lived close to his office and thought a scooter would help him save gas. While on the phone with a friend from across the country, Marcus mentioned his new scooter. There was silence on the other end. "Marcus," his friend asked, "is everything okay?" Marcus was confused. "Yeah, why?" After a bit of awkward discussion, Marcus' friend admitted that where he lives, people buy scooters when their licenses have been revoked for driving under the influence. They had a good laugh about the whole story, but the initial silence was a clue to cultural differences that needed interpretation.

Exploring a person's historical, cultural, and circumstantial context means that we recognize that other people are different than us, even when we may appear to be similar. As Gerkin elaborates, "if the pastoral counselor is a good listener to stories, he or she will soon recognize that there are subtle differences in the way individuals within the same cultural milieu make use of language symbols and images."[10]

2. Recognize and Bridge the Distance

In what ways are you different from the person you are ministering to? Recognizing and bridging distance is especially important when thinking about the complex contextual world of gender. In *Preaching that Speaks to Women*, Alice Mathews argues that pastors need see how their hermeneutics and homiletics should be informed by differences in gender in order to be contextually relevant.[11] While there are clear differences between men and women, "less

> . . . *pastors need see how their hermeneutics and homiletics should be informed by differences in gender in order to be contextually relevant.*

---

10. Gerkin, *Living Human Document*, 27. Gerkin uses the metaphor of "looking over the fence" to describe understanding another person's context (ibid.).

11. Mathews, *Preaching That Speaks*, 15–29.

evident are the possible differences in interests, attitudes, and even vocabularies between a group of men, a group of women, and a mixed audience. Consequently, the tendency in preaching is to think that where gender is concerned, one size fits all."[12]

I remember speaking to a woman who was struggling with boundaries in regards to ministry. Even on the verge of burnout, she still wanted to be available to God. She told me, "I was at an event recently, and the pastor said that we need to stop being selfish and give ourselves away in service to others. It was a great message and I understand his point, but most of us at the event were women. We looked at each other like, 'So we have to give ourselves away even more than we're doing now?' The pastor was really excited to share this with us, but I'm not sure if he realizes that the idea of selfishness is a little different for women than it is for men."

We need to confront our own myths about gender, such as exaggerating the differences between men and women, lumping men and women into broad categories, or seeing gender as the most important gap needing to be bridged. But the distance is not just about gender. We all harbor myths, biases, misconceptions, and ignorance about people of other ages, ethnicities, and values. Bridging the distance involves recognizing the differences between us, not judging people on neutral issues, and finding ways to help people in their context.

3. Identify Possible Patterns and Coding

Grief and loss, addiction, domestic abuse, diagnoses of physical or mental illnesses, childhood sexual trauma, miscarriage, divorce, and depression are all issues that pastors will regularly be asked to address while caring for their congregations. Each of these situations comes with common recognizable symptoms, reliable assessments for discerning their severity, and suggested paths for treatment. Just as we can see patterns in the written texts we read,

12. Ibid.,17.

we should be able to recognize patterns in the human documents we counsel. Both Christian and secular resources can provide useful information gathered from real-life research.

Christians have discerned patterns in human behavior for centuries. Before the rise modern secular psychology, great Christian leaders like the Desert Fathers, John Chrysostom, Gregory the Great, Richard Baxter, John Wesley, and Jonathan Edwards were categorizing common issues and prescribing spiritual care to hurting people. Many Christians in the twentieth century have continued in this tradition. In his book, *The Minister as Diagnostician: Personal Problems in Pastoral Perspective*, Paul Pruyser writes, "pastors, like all other professional workers, possess a body of theoretical and practical knowledge that is uniquely their own, evolved over years of practice by themselves and their forebears."[13] Just as secular psychologists and psychiatrists have created the *Diagnostic and Statistical Manual of Mental Disorders* (DSM), a detailed collection of symptoms and patterns for diagnosis and treatment, so too should pastors have access to well-researched materials to help them triage the common pastoral issues they will be face with in their congregations.[14]

> *Just as we can see patterns in the written texts we read, we should be able to recognize patterns in the human documents we counsel.*

Personality assessments are another way to identify patterns. The Myers-Briggs Type Indicator (MBTI), the Taylor-Johnson Temperament Analysis (T–JTA), and the Minnesota Multiphasic Personality Inventory (MMPI) are popular tools for helping

13. Pruyser, *Minister as Diagnostician*, 10.

14. Some helpful resources from the American Association of Christian Counselors include *The Quick-Reference Guide to Biblical Counseling* by Tim Clinton and Ron Hawkins; *The Quick Reference Guide to Marriage and Family Counseling* by Tim Clinton and John Trent; *The Quick Reference Guide to Counseling Women* by Tim Clinton and Diane Langberg; and *The Quick Reference Guide to Sexuality and Relationship Counseling* by Tim Clinton and Mark Laaser.

identifying patterns in personality. More recently, assessment programs such as the Clifton StrengthsFinder, Prepare/Enrich, and the Five Love Languages have gained popularity in the Christian community.[15] In the same way that understanding biblical genres can help us know what we are reading, familiarity with basic personality types, strengths, and relational styles can help us interpret people.

Patterns and coding are important in pastoral counseling, but we should be careful to avoid simplistic generalizations or premature categorization. Anthropologist Clifford Geertz describes this as the difference between "thin" and "thick" descriptions of people.[16] When we rush to judgment or stereotype people without proper sensitivity to their unique context, we create "thin" descriptions of them. "Thick" descriptions are formed when we take time to listen, explore context, and avoid simplistic diagnoses. For example, a "thin" description of a person with depression might lead a pastor to recommend that the person think positive thoughts, get outside more often, memorize encouraging passages of Scripture, and find a way to serve others. A "thick" description might lead the pastor to suggest some of the above, but the conscientious pastor would also help the person explore any unhealthy beliefs and possible causes of depression, including life transitions, biological issues, relational conflicts, and even familial patterns of diagnosed or undiagnosed neurological imbalances.

Whether we are interpreting biblical texts or living human documents, the third step of interpretation involves taking historical, cultural, and circumstantial context into account. We must attend to this background information to fully understand what is

15. For further details on these programs, please see Wiseman et al., *Living Your Strengths*; Life Innovations, "Overview of Prepare/Enrich," https://www.prepare-enrich.com; Chapman, *Five Love Languages*.

16. Geertz, *Interpretation of Cultures*, 3–13. This is also described as the difference between "characters" and a "characterization" in McKee, *Story*, 100–101.

in the foreground. By entering into a person's world as Christ did ours—lovingly, respectfully, and thoughtfully—we can bridge the distances between us and help them to shape their lives toward God's pattern. As the Bible says: "Do not conform to the pattern of this world, but be transformed by the renewing of your mind. Then you will be able to test and approve what God's will is—his good, pleasing and perfect will" (Rom 12:2).

Prayer

God, thank you creating us all to be unique and different. Help us to recognize the differences between ourselves and those you have given into our care. Guide us as we graciously explore their histories, cultures, and circumstances. May we help them discover that others have shared their struggles and that there are paths that can lead them to you for hope, healing, and holiness. In Jesus' name, Amen.

Main Ideas

- History, culture, and the immediate circumstances of an event can be the most important factors for proper interpretation.

- Understanding the author's motives can help you know how to understand what the author has communicated.

- "Distance" refers to the differences between those we minister to and ourselves.

- Useful information from a person's life can be discovered through a simple inventory or by asking questions to explore context.

- People are all different, but there are patterns in personality and behavior that can assist pastors in ministering to hurting people.

Discussion Questions

1. What insights did you find most significant in this chapter?

2. Why do you believe some people overlook the importance of historical and culture context?

3. Describe the distance between yourself and someone to whom you have recently ministered. What were the main differences between you, and in what ways did you bridge those distances?

4. What kind of influences do past experiences exert on current thoughts, feelings, and decisions?

5. What are some common patterns you see in your ministry of pastoral care and counseling?

Exercise 1: Knowing Your Own Culture

To understand the differences between ourselves and other people, we must know something about our own culture. Create a basic culture profile for yourself by answering the following questions:

1. What is your ethnic or racial background? Do you closely identify with others of the same ethnicity or race?

2. Using Lingenfelter and Mayers' six categories of culture referenced in this chapter, in what ways are your values similar to or different from those of your family, church, or ethnic group?

3. How knowledgeable are you of the thoughts and feelings of the opposite gender? What conversations, relationships, or readings have helped you to be more sensitive to differences between men and women?

4. What is the "culture" of your church (i.e., ethnicity, values, socio-economics, ministry philosophy, aesthetics, etc.)? What is the relationship between your church's culture and the culture(s) of the surrounding community?

Exercise 2: Assessing Distance

Think about a recent or upcoming counseling appointment. Fill in the following chart and pray about what you discover.

	You	Person to whom you are ministering	Distance or differences	Significance this distance may have on your counseling
Age				
Culture				
Gender				
Family Structure				
Personality Type				
Level of Spiritual Maturity				
Other?				

Recommended Reading

Misreading Scripture with Western Eyes: Removing Cultural Blinders to Better Understand the Bible
by E. Randolph Richards and Brandon J. O'Brien

> Written to help interpreters discover and question their biases, this book challenges readers to rethink their pre-understanding of both Scripture and people.

Ministering Cross-Culturally: An Incarnational Model for Personal Relationships
by Sherwood G. Lingenfelter and Marvin K. Mayers

> An accessible introduction to cross-cultural ministry that includes a way to personally assess your cultural values based on a model of twelve contrasting basic values.

Preaching That Speaks to Women by Alice Mathews

> Mathews' book is a practical resource for pastors who need to discover important distinctions between and among women and men.

Hermenuetics: Principles and Processes of Interpretation by Henry A. Virkler

> Virkler offers a great chapter on historical-cultural and contextual analysis, including an insightful treatment of exploring the "spiritual disposition" of the original readers.

Perspectives on the World Christian Movement by the Perspectives Study Program, www.perspectives.org

> Taught at different locations around the world, this course presents God's plan to reach the world and emphasizes the role of historical-cultural context in ministry.

4

What Is the Big Idea?

Interpreting Narrative Genre

Our lives, like the Bible, are filled with stories. Stories involve character, plot, conflict, and resolution. How can understanding the main idea of a story help us make sense of it and know what to do with it?

DAN THOUGHT OVER ALL that Sarah had shared—about her upbringing, her brother's death, her mother at Dix Hill, and her desire to be a Proverbs 31 woman.

"I've been reading and praying more," Sarah continued, "but I just can't get anywhere. It's just not working out for me. I'm not sleeping well. I'm eating all the time."

Sarah's pauses were getting longer. Dan wondered whether Sarah was running out of things to say, or if she was slowly inching toward a revelation. After a few moments, she confessed, "I snap at the kids all the time. My husband too . . . when he's there," she added with a tinge of irritation. She fell silent again, seeming exhausted by what little she had said. "My husband says, 'Just pray more and you'll feel better.' But," she said sadly, "he's not the one with the kids all day . . . " Sarah lapsed into the longest silence yet. Dan sensed something coming.

"I don't want to be weak."

It took a lot of willpower for Dan to hold back from speaking. He reviewed what Sarah had revealed—about growing up with an unstable mother, her brother's death, and the many things she did not seem comfortable talking about. Maybe it was her Southern culture that valued putting up a good front. Dan wondered if this was how she was raising her own family. Her husband sounded somewhat removed. Sarah probably had some high expectations about homeschooling, but maybe she felt she couldn't live up to them. She seemed to have similar expectations about what kind of Christian woman she should be. Dan had a lot of possible issues to explore: depression, grief, marriage, parenting, and her embedded beliefs about God, herself, and the world. There are a lot of pieces to this puzzle, but what is the big picture? What is this woman's story all about?

Life is not a series of random events. Like a great narrative, our lives are like stories. God intends the pieces come together to move us forward. There is purpose and direction, but we face obstacles and conflicts. Only by overcoming these conflicts can our stories come to a resolution. At the climax of our stories, we come face-to-face with what our story is all about—its Big Idea. Following the flow of a narrative and discovering its Big Idea is part of understanding genre. This is the fourth step of interpretation.

What Is Genre?

Authors choose to communicate their message through specific literary forms, and "recognizing the particular genre is the key to understanding."[1] The Bible contains information about God, ourselves, and the world, but "this information comes neither in the form of an encyclopedia, nor as a ready reference manual. God has given us this information in many different forms—narrative, poetry, letters, songs, prophecies, apocalyptic, drama, gospel, wisdom literature, and proverbs."[2]

1. McCartney and Clayton, *Let the Reader Understand*, 155.
2. Adams, *Use of the Scriptures*, 42.

Narratives comprise almost half of the Old Testament and large sections of the New Testament. God's interactions with his people are described in stories—prophets confronted kings with well-crafted stories, and Jesus' primary means for teaching was through stories in the form of parables. The Bible says that Jesus "did not say anything to them without using a parable" (Mark 4:33). Thus, one could argue that narrative is God's preferred method for communicating truth.

Stories are also the primary way we communicate truths about ourselves. James Bryan Smith writes, "When we have a significant experience—one that shapes us—we turn it into a story."[3] These stories may or may not accurately reflect the truth, but they nevertheless shape us. Therefore, understanding the genre of narratives and how to read stories is crucial for our understanding of Scripture and our understanding of people.

> *. . . understanding the genre of narratives and how to read stories is crucial for our understanding of Scripture and our understanding of people.*

Arguably, genre is the first step of interpretation, because without knowing the genre, we cannot understand the author's intent or fully explore the historical-cultural context. In situating genre so far into this method, I am in no way diminishing its importance. Rather, in the practice of pastoral care and counseling, I have found myself "discovering the narrative" as the person seeking help discloses more and more information. As we listen to words, pay attention non-verbal cues, and listen for context, a person's story begins to take shape.

---

3. Smith, *Good and Beautiful God*, 24.

Narratives 101

Many pastors are more comfortable with didactic literature like epistles, which offer clearly lain out propositional truth. As a result, pastors and Bible teachers read narratives looking for characters to state these truths and seeking characters to emulate. While this kind of approach is certainly a valid way to read narratives, there is much more to the stories of the Bible.

Narratives are designed to draw the reader into an experience. Thomas Long explains that "narratives are difficult because of what they are and what they aim to do: texts summon readers and hearers to see themselves as human beings standing in the presence of God."[4] Narratives are more complicated than didactic literature because they demand more from the reader, but all narratives contain the same basic elements. Familiarity with these elements can help us to interpret the stories we read, whether in written or human documents.[5]

1. Characters

Who is the main character in the story? Which other people are involved in the story? What roles do they play in the life of the main character? In regards to biblical interpretation: Next to God, who is the main character of the narrative? What is this character's relationship to God? Who is the antagonist in the story? With regard to pastoral counseling: What is your counselee's relationship with God? Who are the most important or influential people in the life of your counselee?

---

4. Long, *Preaching from Memory*, 23.

5. For more understanding about the elements and structures of narratives see Edwards, *Effective First-Person Preaching;* Ibarra and Lineback, "What's Your Story?" 43–61.

2. Setting

What is the location of the story? When and where does the story take place, and what significance does this have? Regarding biblical interpretation: Does the story take place in Israel, or somewhere else? Is the country at war or enjoying peace? In regards to pastoral counseling: What is the current setting of your counselee's life (i.e., living arrangement, employment, church attendance, relationships, etc.)? Where do they perceive God's presence in their current situation?

3. Inciting Incident

What dramatic event starts the story? What situation upsets the world of the main character and drives him or her to action? In regards to biblical interpretation: What problem has changed the character's world? In what way has God called the main character to action? In regards to pastoral counseling: What has brought the counselee into counseling? What has happened in the counselee's life that has upset his or her world? What has prompted their need for help?

4. Dialogue

What do the main characters say to each other? Is the content of their conversions healthy or unhealthy, biblical or unbiblical? How do these conversations reveal what the characters value? Regarding biblical interpretation: What has God said to the main character? What do the characters say when they talk to God and to each other? In regards to pastoral counseling: What, if anything, does the counselee believe God is saying to them? What is their prayer-life like? To whom does the counselee talk or listen to regularly? Are these conversations healthy and biblical? What were conversations like in the counselee's home of origin?

5. Plot

How does the story move along—positively, negatively, or surprisingly? What is the focus of the story? Is the main character learning something, making a difficult choice, being tested, etc.? In regards to biblical interpretation: What is God trying to do in the main character's life? What is the biblical story about—testing, punishment, redemption, forgiveness? With regard to pastoral counseling: What does the counselee believe God is doing in his or her life? What is the mood of the counselee's life—positive, negative, or always filled with twists and turns?

6. Conflict

What kind of conflict is the main character facing—personal (with themselves), inter-personal (with others), or extra-personal (with natural world)? What was, is, or might be, the "turning point" that will help the character overcome this conflict? In regards to biblical interpretation: Is the character fighting against the flesh, the world, the devil, God, or something else? How can the main character find peace, victory, or holiness? Does the story find resolution? If so, when does it happen? Regarding pastoral counseling: What is the main conflict the counselee is facing? Have they identified the right battle? What must they do, or stop doing, in order to live the life God intends?

Great narratives start with some kind of inciting incident. Joseph has a dream that gets him thrown into a pit by his brothers (Genesis 37), the younger son leaves with his inheritance (Luke 15:12), or King David sees Bathsheba from his balcony (2 Sam 11:2–3). An inciting incident introduces conflict in the character's life. The narrative then follows the character through the ensuing conflict until resolution. Sometimes there are multiple conflicts in a character's life. Moses wrestles with his calling, opposes Pharaoh, and struggles with the Israelites, but all these conflicts reach their climax with the dramatic standoff at the shore of the Red Sea (Exod

14:15–16). Stories tend to reach a dramatic climax right before the conflict is ultimately resolved. Some call this the "winter" of the story or the "dark night of the soul" moment. This is the moment when all seems lost, but when the main character usually overcomes their conflict and the story comes to a peaceful resolution.

While narratives are creative and interesting, it is important to remember that Bible narratives were not primarily written for enjoyment, but for spiritual development. Like all other biblical genres, narratives communicate theological ideas. They contain embedded theology and promote a certain worldview. They should be read as theological history with the clear purpose of influencing the reader to understand something about who God is and how God works.[6]

What Is the "Big Idea?"

Haddon Robinson argues that every story has one "Big Idea."[7] Like the spokes of a wagon wheel, all the different elements of a story come together to point to a central idea. This central idea is what the story is all about and contains the message the author wants to communicate. This organizing idea is usually found in the conflict of the story. Simply put, the main character wrestles with an idea. When the wrestling is done, the story is over. In his book on preaching, Kent Edwards suggests that the Big Idea in biblical narratives can be expressed in two sentences.[8] The first sentence begins with "What happened when . . . ?" This sentence should address the source of conflict in the main character's life. The second sentence answers the first question and contains the resolution of the conflict. These two sentences form the controlling idea of the story. Consider the following examples:

6. Edwards, *Effective First-Person Preaching*, 31. McCartney and Clayton, *Let the Reader Understand*, 225.

7. Robinson, *Biblical Preaching*, 33–50.

8. Edwards, *Effective First-Person Preaching*, 64–71.

- Dan 1: What happened when Daniel and his friends refused to defile themselves by consuming the royal food and wine? God gave them better health and academic success than all of the other students who ate the defiling food.[9]

- 2 Sam 11–12: What happened when David tried to avoid the consequences of his sin with Bathsheba? He discovered God wouldn't let him.

- John 9: What happened when the Pharisees refused to accept Jesus' healing of the blind man? They remained in their spiritual blindness.

Once you have expressed the Big Idea in the form of a two-sentence description of the conflict and resolution, you can shape the Big Idea into a one-sentence, solution-oriented summary. I recommend starting the sentence with the words: "This is the story of a person who . . ." Consider the previous biblical examples:

- Dan 1: This is the story of four young friends who were blessed because they remained faithful.

- 2 Sam 11–12: This is the story of a man who needed to face the sin in his life rather than avoid it.

- John 9: This is the story of highly religious people who could only see clearly by realizing they were blind.

The Big Idea of a narrative is important. Without it, sermons become a wandering series of talking points or moral lessons about parts of the story. The Big Idea helps the interpreter sort through all the contextual information provided and focus teaching and application around the author's intended message. Finding this Big Idea is not an exact science. We can never claim with absolute certainty that we have found the

> *The Big Idea helps the interpreter sort through all the contextual information provided and focus teaching and application around the author's intended message.*

9. Ibid., 66.

exact controlling idea the author intended, but if we follow the basic guidelines for interpreting narratives, we should find ourselves circling the same main ideas.

A word of caution: Sometimes our personal orientation as an interpreter will lead us to read the same idea into texts over and over again. We have all heard pastors preach different texts, but all the while communicating the same main idea. If we find ourselves finding the same Big Idea in every text we are studying, we need to reevaluate the role of our pre-understanding in interpretation.

Shaping the Story

Story-shaping involves reshaping or rephrasing material in order to communicate the Big Idea in ways the listener can understand.[10] Donald Sunukjian illustrates this with the exegesis of Phil 1:3–5. If we read this passage in its written order, it appears to make three statements: (1) "I thank God for you," (2) "I remember you," and (3) "I pray for you and your partnership with me." But the author's thought order reveals something very different. This passage is better understood to be saying, "Whenever I remember you, I remember your partnership with me and this leads me to be thankful and pray for you."[11]

Story-shaping is important when interpreting narratives because stories are not always ordered with a complete chronology. Some narratives are purposely incomplete in their record of events. For example, as opposed to the book of Kings, Chronicles is a shorter and more selective record of Israel's history. Other narratives are complied by topic or theme. Matt 8 contains a grouping of stories organized around Jesus' authority, and 2 Sam 21–24 contains a grouping of stories about David's successes. Sometimes narratives move backward or forward in time, revisiting and retelling events from different perspectives. This literary device, called "recapitulation," is at the center of the debate on how to understand

10. Edwards, "Stories Are for Adults," http://www.preachingtoday.com/skills/themes/stories/storiesareforadults.html.

11. Sunukjian, *Introduction to Biblical Preaching*, 60–61.

the book of Revelation. Whether a narrative is chronologically selective or involves recapitulation, our goal is to determine how the author originally thought of it rather than how it is written.[12]

When people come for counseling, they do not always tell their stories in chronological order. Rather, they highlight important events and group events together in order to make their point. They may tell and retell their stories, emphasizing different aspects. In his book on hermeneutics, Abraham Kuruvilla concludes his examination of narratives by saying, "any narrator of any text has the freedom to prioritize, schematize, and organize his raw material for his express purpose."[13] We must develop skills that allow us to sort through narrative material to find the Big Idea the author is attempting to communicate. This may mean reordering some details or bringing certain story elements (such as cultural details, setting, characters, or dialogue) to the forefront in order to shape the story in a way that allows the narrative to have its intended impact.

Story-shaping should not imply that the original presentation of a narrative is wrong or flawed. Story-shaping is a form of clarification. Considering difficulties like distance and intention, story-shaping helps us retell a narrative to insure that the author's message is clearly understood and communicated.

Narrative Genre in Pastoral Counseling

1. Help Identify the Conflict in a Person's Story

Stories are fueled by conflict. The source of this conflict is often found in the competing beliefs and values within a person. As mentioned previously, we all operate from our own set of core beliefs, or "embedded theology." These beliefs are what we think about God, other people, the world, and ourselves. Conflict arises when our assumptions and core beliefs are challenged, when things

12. Ibid., 56–64.

13. Kuruvilla, "Pericopes, Theology, and Application," 104.

aren't happening in the way they should, or when things are not how we believe they should be. Conflicts develop when our "embedded theology" can no longer help us make sense of the world. Consider the following examples of people expressing conflict in response to their core beliefs or assumptions being challenged:

Statement of Conflict	Core Beliefs or Assumptions
I have been living a good life, so why is this illness happening to me?	Morality brings good health. We can know why bad things happen
I raised my son in the church and now he's gone and joined another religion!	Good parenting leads to godly children. God promises that our children will follow him (Prov 22:6).
I gave thirty years of my life to that company and they just laid me off.	If you work hard and you'll be rewarded. Fairness is owed to us if we are faithful.
I've been praying for God's direction and I'm getting no clarity at all!	Spiritual direction comes through prayer. God always answers our specific prayers.

I recently spoke with a young woman named Susan who was having a hard time making friends. As she told me the story of her life, she mentioned how her family made fun of her when she shared her feelings. As she told me more about growing up, it became clear that over time, and without even knowing it, Susan had developed a set of core beliefs based on "My family doesn't care about my feelings," or "My feelings are wrong," or "People are mean." These core beliefs became Susan's "operational theology." She lived her life believing that "if I share my feelings, then people will make fun of me." Now a grown woman, Susan felt closed, impersonal, and distant. The conflict she was facing was not with other people, but with her own ability to trust people with her feelings and risk being hurt.

Finding and exploring a person's core beliefs is creative work, similar to a storyteller digging beneath the surface of the story to discover characters' motivations and feelings. As such, we do our best work "not with the presenting issues, which are seldom the real issue. Most presenting issues are merely symptomatic of underlying theological issues."[14] In this way, pastors can help people discover their own embedded beliefs and assumptions. As we identify the conflict, we can gently ask, "It sounds like you believe_____. Is that true?" If we find that our counselees' beliefs and assumptions are biblical and healthy, we can reinforce and affirm them. If they are unbiblical or unhealthy, their beliefs and assumptions should be graciously challenged. Challenging and helping a person think through their core beliefs this way is called "deliberative theology."[15]

2. Assist in Finding the Big Idea of the Story

When someone comes to counseling, they are unable to piece together all the elements of their story in way that makes sense. They need help seeing the big picture. They need a "co-author."[16] Drawing on the sociological, anthropological, and literary principles of storytelling, psychologists Michael White and David Epston developed an approach to counseling called narrative therapy.[17] Narrative therapy, like story-shaping, encourages identifying, retelling, and reinterpreting of the elements of a person's story with the goal of helping them discover a new reality. Consider how the following questions might be used in pastoral counseling to help explore a person's story:

14. Barnes, *Pastor as Minor Poet*, 22.
15. Doehring, *Practice of Pastoral Care*, 112–21.
16. Payne, *Narrative Therapy*, 39.
17. See White and Epston, *Narrative Means*.

What brings you here today?	Inciting Incident
When did this start? What other issues are making your current situation difficult?	Setting
What are your current struggles or conflicts? What are your sources of stress?	Conflict
Who are the main people in your life? Where, if anywhere, do you see God in this?	Characters
What are all the different voices in your life saying right now? What, if anything, do you sense God saying to you right now?	Dialogue
Where do you see this situation going? What do you sense God doing?	Plot

The Big Idea revolves around a person's conflict. Once you have identified the conflict, you are closer to finding the Big Idea. For example, the story behind Susan's difficulties making friends revealed that the main conflict centered on Susan's fear of sharing her feelings with others. A possible two-sentence Big Idea to Susan's story might be: "What happens when Susan has the opportunity to get close to new people? She closes up out fear of being hurt." A one-sentence, solution-oriented Big Idea could be: "This is the story of a woman who needs to risk being hurt in order to have satisfying relationships." Consider the story of the man who was having a problem "getting into the Word." Alan's conflict was with his beliefs and assumptions about what quality time with God looks like. A possible two-sentence Big Idea could be: "What happens when Alan begins his personal time with God? He feels defeated because he believes he is not spending enough time in devotions." A one-sentence, solution-oriented Big Idea for Alan might be: "This is the story of a man who must change his expectations in order to spend quality time with God."

Here is another example: Ann was feeling frustrated and depressed about not being able to find a job. As she shared her story with me, Ann mentioned that she did not finish her college degree because of feelings of depression resulting from a history of verbal abuse and high academic demands by her mother. When she thought about work or going back to school, she felt drained and unmotivated. Ann had extra-personal conflict with the job market, but her main conflict was internal—with her mother's criticisms echoing in her head. A possible two-sentence Big Idea for Ann's story could be: "What happens when Ann thinks about her joblessness and dropping out of college? Her mother's negative and demanding criticisms echo in her head." A one-sentence, solution-oriented Big Idea for Ann could be: "This is the story of a woman who must learn to hear God's grace louder than critical voices."[18]

Counselors and pastors who are skilled in interpretation are able to sort through a wide variety of verbal, non-verbal, contextual, and narrative information to isolate and articulate the Big Ideas of the stories they read and hear.

3. Begin to Help Reshape, Recast, Reframe, and Rescript the Story

We are all shaped by our stories. Our stories help us understand who we are, where we have come from, what God has done, and where our lives are going. If we do not interpret stories correctly, we run the risk of misunderstanding God, others, the world, and ourselves. When we realize that "if we all live story-formed

18. This example shows how characters not expressly identified in a narrative (or even alive in the world of the counselee) can still shape a person's story. In Family Systems Theory, they are referred to as "ghosts." Exegetically, this is context and subtext at work. N. T. Wright describes the outside influences of characters on the biblical authors: "Just as King Herod looms over much of the Gospel narratives, so Caesar, the Roman emperor, looms unmentioned over several passages in Paul's works" (Wrights, *Acts, Romans, 1 Corinthians*, 423).

lives, then we are confronted with the question, What stories will shape us?"[19]

In preaching, we assist people in re-storying their lives in a way that aligns with the larger narrative of God's story.[20] Our goal is to help people see God's intention and live their lives accordingly. In pastoral counseling, we assist people to alter the Big Idea of their stories to better align with God's will for them.

Reshaping involves helping people deliberate over their embedded theology. We encourage them to ask themselves: What are my beliefs about God, others, the world, and myself? Are these beliefs biblical? Healthy? Recasting involves helping people examine the influence of others in their story. We encourage them to ask themselves: Who is God using in my life? Are there important people I have excluded from my story? Are there perhaps some I need to exclude? How do I sense God speaking to me? Reframing involves helping people consider new ways of viewing their situation. We encourage them to ask themselves: Is there another way to interpret what is happening to me? Could this bad thing in my life bring about something good? Might this conflict help me grow in some way? Is this relationship problem more about me than the other person? Rescripting involves helping people change the way they talk to God, others, and themselves. We encourage them to ask themselves: How is what I am saying to myself helping or hurting my situation? Am I hearing from God, or am I simply rebroadcasting my own thoughts and feelings in prayer? How can I begin to think, feel, and act in ways that will help me overcome the conflict of my story?

We are not our own (1 Cor 6:19–20). Therefore, we can only make sense of our stories in light of God's presence in our lives. God is the main character of biblical narratives and of our stories as well. God invites us to re-story our conflicted personal narratives and

---

19. Green, *Narrative Reading, Narrative Preaching*, 17.
20. Wright, *Telling God's Story*, 100–101.

encourages us to do this within a community. When we gather with other believers for worship, prayer, study, and the application of God's Word—in short, when we open our lives to trusted Christian brothers and sisters—God's intention is that our lives be shaped around the gospel. Whether the text is written or human, our desire is to help people re-author their lives around Jesus Christ and his redemption. As Allender reminds us:

> When I study and understand my life story, I can then join God as a coauthor. I don't have to settle for merely being a reader of my life; God calls me to be a *writer of my future*.[21]

Prayer

God, thank you being the author of life and all great stories. Help us understand how to read and retell stories so we can allow your Word to come alive in our lives. Open our eyes to the details of our stories and the stories of those to whom we minister so we will not miss your presence and voice. May we help each other to see our lives as part of your great story of Jesus Christ, for your glory alone. In Jesus' name, Amen.

Main Ideas

- One of the most common genres of the Bible is narrative.
- Most people communicate about themselves through stories.
- Understanding the basic elements of story can help us interpret Scripture and minister to people.
- The Big Idea of a story is usually embedded in the main character's conflict.

21. Allender, *To Be Told*, 3, emphasis Allender's.

- Stories communicate powerful theological ideas in indirect ways that shape the actions of those in the narrative.

Discussion Questions

1. What did you find most significant in this chapter?

2. What makes narratives so difficult to interpret and preach?

3. What is the Big Idea of the last movie you watched or book you read?

4. What is a Big Idea in your life? Write it in two-sentence and one-sentence form.

5. How, specifically, does God use Christian fellowship among believers to help reshape, recast, reframe, and rescript the stories of our lives?

Exercise 1: Finding the Big Idea of a Narrative

Reread the counseling vignettes between Pastor Dan and Sarah. Based on what you have learned so far, attempt to identify Sarah's conflict and the Big Idea of her story. Consider the following questions:

1. What is the inciting incident of Sarah's story? Who are the characters in her story? Which characters are most important in Sarah's story? Where is God in her story?

2. What is Sarah's embedded theology—her beliefs about God, family, mental illness, weakness, etc.?

3. What are the main conflicts in Sarah's life? Would you label them as extra-personal, personal, or inner conflicts? Which conflict seems to be at the root of her struggle?

4. What would you consider to be the Big Idea of her story? How would you complete the following sentence: "This the story of a woman who . . ."?

5. How would you begin helping Sarah reshape, recast, reframe, and rescript her narrative?

Exercise 2: A Narrative of Your Own

Think about the important events in your life. Which stories have had the most significant impact on your life (i.e., a death, conversion, meeting your spouse, changing careers, or losing a dream)? Consider one of your stories and answer the following questions:

1. What was the inciting incident of this story? What started this story in your life, and who were the main characters involved? What roles did they play?

2. What kind of conflict was at the core of your story? What were you struggling with?

3. What was your embedded theology? What beliefs guided you as you went through this story? Which beliefs were accurate and biblical? Did you hold any beliefs that were not accurate interpretations of reality? In what ways did you "misread" your life during this time? Did your beliefs change?

4. What was the Big Idea of your story? How would you complete the following sentence: "This was the story of a person who . . ."?

5. In what ways was your story reshaped, recast, reframed, or rescripted? How did this occur? Who helped you to see or interpret things differently?

Recommended Reading

Effective First-Person Biblical Preaching: The Steps from Text to Sermon by J. Kent Edwards

> Edwards presents a simple, thorough, step-by-step approach to preaching biblical narratives. This book is a must-read for anyone seeking to understand how to interpret and communicate stories.

Biblical Preaching: The Development and Delivery of Expository Messages by Haddon Robinson

> This classic work on preaching explains basic hermeneutics and homiletics, but is most useful in advocating "big idea expository preaching."

The Good and Beautiful God: Falling in Love with the God Jesus Knows by James Bryan Smith

> Based on the premise that our stories run (and sometimes ruin) us, Smith offers a spiritual formation approach to aligning our narratives with Jesus' greater story.

The Practice of Pastoral Care: A Postmodern Approach by Carrie Doehring

> Doehring explains "embedded" versus "deliberative" theology and how to help people explore their beliefs through careful listening and skilled questioning.

Narrative Pastoral Counseling by Burrell David Dinkins

> This brief and readable book integrates narrative therapy with solution-focused counseling from a Christian perspective.

5

What Do We Do Now?

Finding Meaning-full Applications

We want change. Finding meaning in written and human texts should lead us to see things in new ways. How does proper interpretation lead to practical life changes?

DAN WAITED A MOMENT for Sarah's admission of weakness to sink in before responding.

"Sarah, I want to thank you for coming to see me. It takes a lot of courage to share what you've shared with me. And I'm glad you've found this church to be a safe place. We're grateful to have you."

"Thank you, Pastor."

"You're welcome." Dan replied. "If it's okay, I'd like to take a moment and just see if I've understood you correctly. I'd like to repeat back some things I've heard from you and maybe offer a few small thoughts so we can talk through how God may be working here. Is that okay?"

"Yes, please," Sarah said, "That's why I'm here."

"Well, I'm really sorry to hear about your brother's death. That's terrible for anyone to go through, especially someone taking his own life. So there seems to be some very painful, but completely normal, grief going on here, and I'd like to make sure you're getting support for that. But it sounds like your brother's death has stirred up quite a bit more inside you."

"Yes, that's right," Sarah agreed.

"You mentioned how this has got you thinking about your mom. And it sounds like you're mom had some problems. I'm not sure what was going on there, but I suppose Dix Hill was a psychiatric hospital?" She nodded. "That must have been very difficult for your whole family. It also sounds like maybe that's something people didn't really talk about in the area or time you grew up."

"No," she replied. "It was embarrassing."

"That's kind of how you were raised? If there was a serious problem like that, you didn't talk about it?"

"I guess so."

"Sarah, is that what the 'spanner in the works' thing means?"

"Oh, yeah," she laughed, "It's just something we said. It's like when you make something worse by stirring up trouble—I guess that's why I never mentioned any of this before!"

"Wow," Dan chuckled, "I hadn't heard that one before." Sarah smiled as Dan went on more seriously, "So, if I'm understanding this right, it's really hard for you to talk about difficulties like mental illness?"

Sarah paused. "Yes."

"Suicide too, I would guess." Sarah nodded again.

"Sarah," Pastor Dan continued, "It seems you have a lot on your plate right now, what with your marriage, the kids, and losing your brother. You're having a hard time sleeping; your eating habits are off. And just now while we were talking, you seemed to drift away at times."

"Yeah," she admitted. "It's like I can't concentrate."

"And it seems like you feel that if you were a better Christian you could just get through this without asking anyone for help and be that Proverbs 31 woman."

"Yes!" Sarah agreed. "That's exactly what I want."

"But . . . you feel weak?"

"Yes."

"And you don't want to be weak." Sarah shook her head. Dan considered a moment before asking, "What does it mean to you to be weak?" Tears came to Sarah's eyes. Dan waited for the space of a few heartbeats. It felt endless. "Was your mom weak?" Dan asked quietly. Sarah nodded, her eyes welling up. "Sarah," Dan asked, "do you feel like if you ever allow yourself to be weak, you'll be just like your mom?"

"I've never felt like this before," Sarah answered. "I don't want to let God down. I don't want to let my family down. I don't want to end up in some crazy hospital."

"Sarah," Dan said, with understanding in his voice, "Thank you so much for being so honest with what's going on in your mind and heart. You've gone through many losses and you're struggling with some painful memories. I think that over the years, you have come to believe that being 'weak' is a bad thing. I'd like us to spend a few minutes talking about what being weak means to you and what the Bible says about weakness. I hope you'll find that it is possible to feel all the things you're feeling, and that you don't have to be afraid."

In counseling Sarah, Dan used active listening, empathy, and articulation. He was able to repeat back to Sarah what he had heard to clarify her meaning and help her get much-needed perspective. He was cautious in summarizing her story, always open to being corrected. He had listened intentionally to her history, saw how her culture shaped her thinking, and sorted through all the elements of her story to get to the heart of her conflict. She was struggling with weakness. The Big Idea of her story was something like: "What happens when Sarah feels like she is weak? She is afraid she will become powerless like her mother." A one-sentence, solution-oriented Big Idea could be: "This is the story of a woman who will only find the strength she needs when she can be weak before God."

Having uncovered Sarah's Big Idea, what should Dan do now? The four previous steps of interpretation have led us here: to application. But application is not a random set of ideas aimed at addressing small points in Sarah's story. True application comes from the meaning of the text. In order to help people experience true and lasting change, they must have "meaning-full" applications. This is the fifth step of interpretation.

What Is Meaning-full Application?

Application should be derived from the author's original intended meaning. This is at the heart of the historical-grammatical method of interpretation. Thus, meaning-full application is when our application comes directly from the original author's meaning. Unfortunately, the application of Scripture is often quite haphazard. Many applications of Scripture, though theologically sound and practically virtuous, have little or no connection to the point the author was trying to make. It is not uncommon for Christians to read Scripture, note important words, be reminded of theological truths, and even sense God speaking as they read and pray over the Bible, but this is no guarantee that they are understanding the meaning of the text or applying it.

I am reminded of conversation with a godly woman who was passionate about Bible memorization. I confessed that I had a hard time remembering Scripture. She told me, "God will help you do it because the Bible says, 'The memory of the just is blessed.'" I found her convincing and I began to memorize more Scripture. Only years later did I reread the text she quoted. It reads, "The memory of the just is blessed: but the name of the wicked shall rot" (Prov 10:7 KJV). This passage is not about memorization; it is about reputation. Is it true that God will help us remember Scripture? Yes. Is it good to remember Scripture? Yes. Should we encourage people to remember Scripture? Yes. Are any of these readings what the original author likely intended us to conclude from this passage? No. The application had no connection to the meaning of the text.

If we don't have a clear idea of the meaning of the text, we risk never applying the text at all. The applications we do create, although biblical, may not have any connection to the text we are referencing. In the worst cases, we create applications that can completely contradict the author's point. Meaning-full application is application that comes directly from the meaning of the text. Whether we call it application, implication, significance, or relevance (and each of these terms have important nuances), meaning-full application is how we make the author's message meaningful in our daily lives. Finding meaning-full application begins with the author's Big Idea.

From Big Idea to Timeless Truth

The first part of application involves locating the Timeless Truth in the Big Idea of the passage. Every text has it's own unique historical, cultural, and circumstantial context, but beneath this there is truth that is relevant for all people and all times. The interpreter's goal is to isolate the timeless, trans-cultural idea of a text.[1] This Timeless Truth is the trans-cultural idea to which the Big Idea is pointing. Sometimes called the "take-home truth" or "homiletical idea," we can think of a text's Timeless Truth as a short phrase or idea that lends itself to easy application for a broad audience.

For example, in the previous chapter's discussion of Daniel 1, it was suggested that the Big Idea could be: "What happened when Daniel and his friends refused to defile themselves by consuming the royal food and wine? God gave them better health and academic success than all of the other students who ate the defiling food." The suggested one-sentence solution-oriented summary was: "This is the story of four young friends who were blessed because they remained faithful." Edwards suggests that the Timeless Truth could be: "God honors faithfulness."[2] This Timeless Truth is not only true of Daniel's story, but is a principle found throughout Scripture and is relevant for us all.

I have suggested that the Big Idea of 2 Samuel 11–12 could be: "What happened when David tried to avoid the consequences

1. Virkler, *Hermenuetics*, 407–25.

2. Edwards, *Effective First-Person Preaching*, 67–68.

of his sin with Bathsheba? He discovered God wouldn't let him."
The one-sentence solution-oriented summary might be: "This is
the story of a man who needed to face the sin in his life rather than
avoid it." Perhaps a Timeless Truth could be: "Your sins will find
you out." Some of the best Timeless Truths are expressed simply
and proverbially in other places in Scripture. A great example of
a Timeless Truth can be created from Joseph's declaration in Gen
50:20: "What man means for evil, God uses for good." This relates
directly to the popular Timeless Truth of Rom 8:28, "in all things
God works for the good of those who love him, who have been
called according to his purpose." Timeless Truths sort through all
the details of a story and translate the controlling idea into a message that can relate to everyone.[3] Timeless Truths remind us that
we are not alone in what we are facing; others have been there and
discovered truth that helped them.

Bible stories were written by an eternal God to communicate
theological truths to all generations (John 20:31, Rom 15:4, 1 Cor
10:11). Sometimes these truths are communicated positively, at
other times negatively. For example, the story of Jephthah and his
daughter in Judg 11 is a chal-
lenging passage to preach, but
it becomes simpler if we look
for the Big Idea and Timeless
Truth of the story. Jephthah, a
military leader desperate for a
great victory, makes a vow to
sacrifice the first thing that
comes forth from his tent if he
returns home successful. After his military triumph, his daughter
comes out from his tent to greet him. If we follow the main elements of the narrative, the story illustrates what people do when
they don't trust God; that is, they make rash vows and commit

> *Timeless Truths remind us
> that we are not alone is what
> we are facing; others have
> been there and discovered
> truth that helped them.*

3. The approach to locating Timeless Truth proposed in this book most
closely resembles that of "principalization" advocated in Kaiser, "Principilizing Model." For equally compelling approaches to locating Timeless Truth, see
Vanhoozer, "Drama-of-Redemption Model"; Kuruvilla, "Pericopes, Theology,
and Application."

senseless, sinful acts. The Big Idea could be: "What happened when Jephthah realized he had made a reckless, faithless vow to God? He kept his vow, thereby sinning against God." A one-sentence summary could be: "This is the story of a man who was more faithful to his vow than to God." Its Timeless Truth could be: "Don't make vows, just obey God." This principle can also be found in other instances throughout the Bible (Matt 5:33–37; Jas 5:12). Timeless Truths offer us a simple spiritual principle upon which to build real-life application.

Moving from Timeless Truth to Application

The meaning of a text is constant, but applications of that text to a person's life can be myriad. As a general rule, a text has only one meaning, but it can be applied in different ways at different times. When I think about the relationship between the meaning of a text and its application, I imagine a target. At the center of the target is the simple, concise, and most specific way of explaining the author's intended meaning. As we move farther away from the center of the target, our applications range farther from the author's meaning. Sometimes, the application of a text has nothing to do with the meaning of the text. I refer to these as "off the target."

We must work to stay as close as possible to the author's intended meaning and the Big Idea of any story. This can be difficult because "Narratives work at different levels. Any good story will have multiple story lines that branch off from the main plot, often, but not always, to return. Narratives are consistently filled with non-narrative material, but such material falls within—and must be interpreted within the framework, the deep structure, or the broader story."[4] The Jephthah narrative is a cautionary tale about oaths, not about girls saying goodbye to their hopes of marriage. Daniel's narrative is about the rewards that come from being faithful to God, not how all-vegetable diets can improve your health. Joseph's narrative is about how even the worst situation can lead

4. Wright, *Telling God's Story*, 80.

to blessing when you are close to God, not practical tips on how to avoid being seduced by older women. We stay "on target" when our application flows as closely from the author's intention as possible.

Application comes in many forms. Evangelical sermons often contain a strong push toward outward action, but not all narratives are designed to do this. Not all Scripture implies something for us to "do."[5] Pratt suggests that narratives have three potential kinds of applications—informative (something to know), directive (something to do), and/or affective (something to feel).[6] In interpretation, we sort through all the narrative material, locate the Big Idea, identify the Timeless Truth, and discern from this understanding what the author wants us to think, do, or feel.

Contextualization and "Turning"

Helping people incorporate Timeless Truth into their lives is called "contextualization." It is the "core of biblical narrative, which asks the reader to apply lessons to one's own situation . . . Narrative demands a reaction to the drama itself. Therefore, we cannot read it without reliving and applying the conflicts and lessons."[7] In contextualization, our goal is take the narrative material and operationalize it in non-narrative ways. Here we ask: "What would this Timeless Truth look like in my life?"

If the Daniel narrative teaches that "God honors faithfulness," then we might ask, "In what specific ways is our faithfulness being challenged?" or, "In what ways has God honored our faithfulness in the past?" or even, "What do we need to be, do, or not do to remain faithful to God?" If the Jephthah narrative teaches, "Don't make vows, just obey God," then we might ask, "In what ways do vows complicate our obedience?" or, "How did Jephthah's vow make God feel?" or, "How can we avoid making promises that we can't or shouldn't keep?"

5. Gibson and Arthurs, "Mood Isn't Always Imperative," www.gordon-conwell.edu/resources/Archives.cfm.

6. Pratt, *He Gave Us Stories*, 318–20.

7. Osborne, *Hermeneutical Spiral*, 220.

When a narrative is contextualized into our lives, our understanding is reshaped and enlarged by the story. The task of the preacher is to bring audiences into the world of the text, recreating the story for the congregation. Listeners are then emotionally affected by their experience of the story and invited to apply its theological truths to their own context. In his book of preaching narratives, John Wright calls this "a rhetoric of turning."[8] On the deepest convictional level, people are challenged to re-narrate their world. Whether informative, directive, or affective, we must help turn "the narratives of the individual and the nation into the narrative of the people of God through Jesus Christ by the power of the Spirit."[9]

For this "turning" to happen, we must help people identify the barriers that prevent them from applying the text to their lives. These barriers can be theological, cultural, informational, linguistic, psychological, emotional, physical, or spiritual. Thus, "the expositor must decide how to eliminate as many of the audience's barriers to textual and theological understanding and belief as appropriate within the available time."[10] Barriers are anything that can confuse, complicate, or make it difficult to apply the meaning of a text to a person's life. In our preaching and pastoral counseling, we must honestly acknowledge and address any objections, challenges, and problems people have when they think about application.

Finally, authentic and lasting application takes time and requires patience. When the gospel was first preached, some came to faith immediately and others wanted to hear more later (Acts 17:32). Timothy was commanded to correct, rebuke, and encourage "with great patience and careful instruction" (2 Tim 4:2). The imagery used throughout the Bible for spiritual growth is that of physical and biological development (1 Cor 3:1–3; John 2:12–14). Many pastors have a strong sense of urgency. They want to see people make decisions and change quickly. Nevertheless, pastors

8. Wright, *Telling God's Story*, 77–104.

9. Ibid., 79.

10. Ralston, "Showing the Relevance," 306.

must offer clear and simple suggestions for contextualization while recognizing that the real work of turning is done over time by the individuals themselves as directed by the Holy Spirit.

Meaning-full Application in Pastoral Counseling

1. Move from Big Idea to Timeless Truth

In the counseling session with Dan and Sarah, I suggested that the Sarah's Big Idea could be: "What happens when Sarah feels like she is weak? She is afraid she will become powerless like her mother." Sarah's one-sentence, solution-oriented Big Idea could be: "This is the story of a woman who will only find the strength she needs when she can be weak before God." Sarah's conflict centered on her fear of weakness. The solution involved needing to hear God's voice. After considering what the Bible says about these issues, a Timeless Truth for Sarah's story might be: "We can only be strong when we let God into our weakness." Perhaps your mind went to the same text as mine did. The Bible tells us, "My grace is sufficient for you, for my power is made perfect in weakness" (2 Cor 12:9). When Paul realized that his "weakness" was being used to lead Paul to be more dependent upon God, he concluded, "when I am weak, then I am strong" (2 Cor 12:10).

Sarah was dealing with extreme grief and serious life transitions. These difficulties call for love, listening, and presence—not fixing. With a supportive community, she will be helped to heal and move through the grief process. She may also be experiencing the effects of strong biochemical issues inherited from her mother, which her brother may have also suffered from. If clinical depression runs in Sarah's family, this might be a good opportunity for a helpful referral to a professional who can address these medical issues. But Dan has a special role in Sarah's life. As Sarah's pastor, Dan is the person she has sought out for help in interpreting her life. Dan can gently and personally guide her to reflect on how God uses weakness to hold and mold us. While Dan might have preached this message by carefully exploring the written text and then declaring it's powerful truth to the congregation, in pastoral counseling, Dan must sensitively explore the human text of Sarah's story. Through careful listening, asking insightful questions, and thoughtful discussion, Sarah can be invited to consider how a new theology of weakness might change the way she looks at her situation.

Consider the story of Alan, who was having difficulties with "getting into the Word." I suggested that the Big Idea of his story could be: "What happens when Alan begins his personal time with God? He feels defeated because he believes he is not spending enough time in devotions." A one-sentence, solution-oriented Big Idea for Alan might be: "This is the story of a man who must change his expectations in order to spend quality time with God." Alan's conflict centered on feeling defeated about the time he spends with God. The solution involves changing how he measures his devotional life with God. What is a Timeless Truth that will help Alan? I can relate to Alan's struggle with not spending enough time with God. Several years ago I spoke with my mentor about a particularly dry period in my spiritual life. After some patient listening, he asked questions about my schedule, how I learn, and what refreshes me. Then he offered the following advice: "You know, Jason, I don't think the Bible contains any specific rules or expectations about how much time you put in. I think it depends on what you get out of that time. Psalm 1 tells us that there is a blessing on those who delight in the Word day and night. I think that means that we should spend time with God and the Bible every day. Maybe you could experiment with having one meaningful encounter with God's Word each day. Don't think about the time or the amount of Scripture, think about your experience with God." The Timeless Truth he gave me could be equally helpful to someone like Alan: "God wants our hearts, not our clocks."

Timeless Truths can come from Scripture, but we can also we see them elsewhere. Similar to the patterns and coding discussed earlier, Erik Erickson provides an example of Timeless Truths about human development, arguing that everyone, from infancy to mature adulthood, wrestles with eight psychosocial crises.[11] Pastoral theologian Donald Capps correlates these with the timeless "deadly sins" listed below:[12]

Stages of Life	Age	Timeless Developmental Conflicts	Deadly Sins
Infancy	0–1	Mistrust versus Trust	Gluttony
Early Childhood	1–3	Shame/Doubt versus Autonomy	Anger
Play Age	3–5	Guilt versus Initiative	Greed
School Age	5–12	Inferiority versus Industry	Envy
Adolescence	12–18	Identity Confusion versus Identity	Pride
Young Adulthood	18–40	Isolation versus Intimacy	Lust
Adulthood	40–65	Stagnation versus Generativity	Apathy
Mature Adulthood	65+	Despair versus Integrity	Melancholy

Timeless Truths help us see through the complicated details of life. They are the simple principles at the center of life's struggles. They help us see where we are and where we need to go. They are found in Scripture, scientific inquiry, and nature, and myriad other places. In pastoral counseling, we help people reinterpret an otherwise confusing or meaningless personal story by helping them to find Timeless Truth and assisting them with its application.

11. Erikson, *Identity and the Life Cycle*, 177–78.
12. Capps, *Deadly Sins and Saving Virtues*.

2. Look for Applications and Barriers to Change

Application can involve changing our thinking (information), starting or stopping actions (direction), or experiencing feelings (affection). If, through our pastoral counseling, people come to realize that their embedded theology contains incomplete data, erroneous theology, or misinformation, then application may be primarily "informative." Informative applications involve helping people discover God through changing thoughts and beliefs. This is normally where pastors thrive. The approach is similar to traditional preaching—providing new information, biblical references, and alternative ways of thinking to help people reframe their perspective so they can think and act differently. For this reason, many pastors tend to favor informative applications in their approach to counseling.

When people are wrestling with difficult decisions, managing responsibilities, or making choices, "directive" applications may prove most helpful. Directive applications involve helping people discover what God is doing in their lives by thinking through choices and adopting new behaviors. Many pastors see themselves as spiritual advice-givers or pastoral problem-solvers. Pastors who are highly action-oriented tend to favor directive applications.

If a person's story involves losses, stress, or traumatic experiences, "affective" applications may be the most helpful form of ministry. Affective applications involve helping people discover God by acknowledging and exploring their feelings and relationships. Pastors who place a high value on emotions and healing interpersonal relationships tend to favor affective applications.

Different situations call for different applications. Therefore, pastors should remember and be ready to use all three kinds of applications in their pastoral counseling. This may be an added challenge for evangelical pastors, who are trained and chosen for their academic, theological, and expositional gifts, but may struggle with feelings and emotions. Pastors who favor information and direction must grow in the affective aspect of their pastoral care and counseling. Discerning people's feelings, setting the emotional tone of ministry, and developing genuine empathy are essential for shepherding God's people through life's hurts. Application is empowered by the emotional and spiritual availability of the pastor's presence.

But application cannot happen without the removal of barriers. We can help people identify potential barriers to spiritual development by asking them, "What do you think will be the hardest part about implementing this new way of looking at things?" or, "What do you think will be the biggest challenge to doing things differently?" or, "What will be most difficult about this new way of feeling?" Without thinking through potential barriers this way, application may not happen. Just like in preaching, we should spend time helping people think through what will prevent, hinder, or challenge them in applying the Timeless Truth in their lives.

What does application and removing barriers look like? Alan was having a problem "getting into the Word." His Timeless Truth involved "giving God his heart, not his clock." Alan's informative applications might involve expanding his understanding of devotional time. There are many biographies, books, and devotionals that emphasize brief, contemplative experiences with God. With more information about differences in devotional reading, Alan may be able to more graciously and meaningfully connect with God. Directive applications may include a commitment to experimenting with his devotional time, trying different locations or lengths of time for prayer, and setting goals for "getting into the Word." This new information and directed experimentation will likely lead to new feelings. Affective applications would involve helping Alan figure how to interpret the different feelings he will experience. For example, what should Alan do if he feels like his devotional time did not produce the spiritual feelings he had expected? Alan could also be encouraged to challenge his negative feelings. After spending time reading and praying, he could be encouraged to journal his feelings and look for positive feelings about God and faith. Exploring potential applications with Alan and asking him about what barriers he anticipates will help Alan more effectively apply the Timeless Truth to his life.

In Sarah's situation, her informative application involves reframing her understanding of weakness. She has come to believe that weakness is a negative force that destroys families, creates shame, and fuels denial. Sarah should be encouraged to begin challenging her core beliefs about weakness, including studying what the Bible says on the subject. Her upbringing has given her an unbiblical worldview that needs to change. Directive applications might include talking honestly about her past and present struggles as well as encouraging Sarah to get some professional help to make sure there are no underlying medical or psychiatric concerns. Affective applications may be the most difficult for Sarah, because she will have to begin accepting her weakness, fear, and feelings of helplessness. She will need permission and opportunity to express her feelings without judgment. This can happen with other people, but inviting Sarah to experiment with her feelings in prayer would be a potentially healing spiritual prescription from her pastor. As Sarah works through these different applications for herself, she may begin to feel more empathy for her mother, whom Sarah had spent years casting as the "crazy person" in her life. As Sarah begins to accept her own weaknesses, she may feel the need to recast her mother in a new role—a fellow sufferer.

3. Be Patient and Encourage Steady Growth

Real transformation takes time. Many evangelical pastors expect immediate "buy in" after preaching a great sermon, but even instant agreement doesn't mean real change will happen, for "It takes time and patience to help people alter the direction of their lives."[13] The same is true in pastoral counseling. People recognize pastoral authority and will want to affirm that the pastor has helped them, but sometimes this impulse is just to make the pastor feel better. We don't need to feel better. We must be committed to honest and humble ministry that acknowledges that the most significant

13. Osborne, *Hermeneutical Spiral*, 450.

problems in life are not solved with quick fixes, Bible quoting, or a couple of action steps.

Encouraging patient and steady growth does not mean that pastors must commit to long-term counseling with their congregation members. My own approach is to meet with a person one time, use the Five Steps of Interpretation, and then refer them to an appropriate ministry, counselor, or lay leader to help with the informative, directive, or affective applications we discover. I then follow up with them throughout their process to reinforce, support, or redirect them in their growth.

> *We must be committed to honest and humble ministry that acknowledges that the most significant problems in life are not solved with quick fixes, Bible quoting, or a couple of action steps.*

We all want big changes, powerful insights, and life-altering decisions. We will experience these things, but our focus should be on the small changes and realistic tasks that we can accomplish, celebrate, and reinforce. The metaphor of the shepherd is a good reminder to pastors that their greatest ministry of guidance will occur over time and through regular loving influence and instruction, not occasional powerful sermons or dramatic power encounters.

It is also important to place the ultimate responsibility for application on the individual. We cannot do the work for people. Psychological studies show that significant behavioral changes are most successful when made by people participating in the process. Don't tell counselees what to do. Suggest ideas, but then ask them what a solution would look like for them specifically. This is "indirect application."[14] Silence can be helpful in this final step of application. As you explore applications and barriers to change, allow for silence and time for thinking. Although it is not often taught to us in our preaching classes, silence is a rhetorical tool.[15] Creating

14. Ibid., 446.

15. Glenn and Ratcliffe, *Silence and Listening.*

this kind of "meaningful silence" allows spiritual space for thinking, feeling, and direction. We cannot assume that people will take the necessary reflective time to ponder application when they leave us, so it is best to incorporate silence into our pastoral counseling. Meaningful silence invites people to have a personal experience with God in our presence. Silence also tests our trust in God and our own patience, for it allows us the freedom to sense how the Holy Spirit is moving someone in a particular direction and forces us to wait on God to illuminate, direct, and come alongside the hurting people who have come to us for pastoral counseling.

In examining ourselves, listening intentionally, being sensitive to context, helping people retell and reshape their narratives, and discovering the application of the Timeless Truths to which God is pointing them, all the pieces of the interpretive process come together as both an art and a science. With skill and creativity, we can help people understand how they fit into God's larger story and encourage them to play their individual part:

> You can think of the whole of God's work in the world as a series of "acts." You've been given the first acts in the Scriptures. You are in the next to last act, which is still being written, and the final act begins in the future when the Lord returns. You know the drama. You know the story. You know where it's going to end up. Now lay it out. Play out your own role on the basis of what God has revealed in the Scriptures. It's sort of like an impromptu piece of jazz. You know the theme; pick it up and play it. In other words, live out the story in obedience to God.[16]

Prayer

God, thank you for making true change possible—in our thoughts, actions, and emotions. Help us know how we should live our lives as we come to know you. Give us the direction we need so our

16. Bruce Waltke quoted in Guthrie, *Read the Bible*, 92.

107

next steps will not be false starts, quick fixes, or self-deceptions. We want to be transformed into the image of your Son so that we can live this mission you gave to him and to us. Thank you for your patience and grace as we grow into that calling. In Jesus' name, Amen.

Main Ideas

- The interpreter's goal is to isolate the timeless, trans-cultural idea of a text.

- The meaning of a text is constant, but a text may offer multiple layers of significance or various applications to different people in different situations.

- Biblical texts and stories have embedded implications by which the author communicates information, direction, or affection.

- We must help people recognize and work to overcome any barriers that may hinder their application of the text.

- Pastors must be patient and encourage steady growth because some changes take time.

Discussion Questions

1. What did you find most significant in this chapter?

2. Meaning is constant, but applications can vary. Why is this an important distinction?

3. What is an example of a Timeless Truth that has helped you through a difficult time?

4. Why is application so important in the interpretive process?

5. Why are people uncomfortable with silence? In what ways do you (or can you) incorporate silence into your pastoral counseling ministry? Into your preaching ministry?

Exercise 1: The Timeless Truth of the Vignette

Having reviewed the counseling vignette at the beginning of each of the chapters, answer the following questions:

1. Do you agree with the Big Idea and Timeless Truth suggested in this chapter? If not, what would you suggest as a Timeless Truth for Sarah?

2. What informative, directive, or affective applications would you suggest to Sarah?

3. What barriers do you think Sarah will face as she attempts to implement changes in her life?

Exercise 2: Timeless Truths in Scripture

Scripture is filled with Timeless Truths that help align our lives with God's will. Spend some time writing out the clearest Timeless Truths you find in Scripture. Some may be direct quotations from the Bible, while others may be your own paraphrases.

Final Thoughts

Exegeting People

WHEN I FIRST STARTED to see the connection between hermeneutics and pastoral counseling, I asked myself, "What if pastors studying Scripture and counselors helping people are really doing the same thing? What if they are both trying to understand two different kinds of documents—written and human? Is it possible that the same set of skills used to read written documents (hermeneutics) could be used to read human documents (pastoral counseling)?" My hope is that your answer to these questions is a resounding "Yes!"

Hermeneutics, homiletics, pastoral care, and counseling share a common foundation in the field of "interpretation." Pastors, psychologists, and theologians have seen this connection for years. David Fairchild, pastor and church planter, writes:

> The principles we use to best understand the text of Scripture and thus know Christ, who is revealed in Scripture, are not followed when we attempt to get to know people . . . To exegete is to draw out, to eisegete is to put in. We often come to the text to put in what we want the text to say. It is no wonder that we do that same in our relationships, even the ones we consider dear and close . . . How much better a pastor, husband, and father would I be if I spent more time working to understand what it is that someone is thinking, saying, and feeling rather than trying to get them to think, say, and feel what I believe is important?[1]

1. Fairchild, "Exegeting vs. Eisogeting People."

In his book on hermeneutics, Joseph Coleson argues that "interpretation" is the common ground between reading texts and understanding people. He explains:

> We all interpret. We interpret when we listen. You know the difference between sincere agreement and sarcastic or even angry disagreement just by the tone of voice of the one speaking to you. If you're in the presence of the one with whom you are speaking, your mind interprets both what you hear and what you see. What you see is often called body language, and it can be very important to correct interpretation. We also interpret when we read. In fact, it's impossible to read without interpreting.[2]

Dietrich Bonhoeffer likewise argued that counseling souls flows naturally from the call to preach, but with one important difference:

> Caring for souls is a proclamation to the individual which is part of the office of preaching . . . it is related to the office of proclamation but not identical to it. In this process of spiritual care . . . the pastor's task is to listen and the parishioner's is to talk . . . for only after a long period of listening is one able to preach appropriately.[3]

We do not have the try to be great preachers *and* great counselors. Our aim should be to be great interpreters! The documents change—from written to human—but we can approach both with the same respect, attention, humility, and skills. Each kind of document helps us hone our interpretive skills, making us more effective in our treatment of the other.

One Thing Every Expert Interpreter Needs

Some texts are easier to read and understand than others. Some passages almost preach themselves, while other require hours of toilsome study. The same is true in pastoral counseling. But there

2. Coleson, *Treasure the Word*, 16.
3. Bonhoeffer, *Testament to Freedom*, 179.

is one attribute great exegetes and great counselors share in common: curiosity. As Robert Dykstra reminds us, "Seminarians and seasoned pastors alike sometimes comment on the tensions between their ministries of preaching and pastoral care, rightly noting that these two tasks require seemingly contradictory ways of approaching or communicating with their parishioners . . . what these two important parts of a pastor's calling have in common is the pastor's personal willingness to pursue enticing leads and follow a childlike curiosity to discover the message in biblical texts as well as human circumstances."[4]

Curiosity drives our desire to learn and understand. We are not doing true exegesis if we are reading or listening only to reinforce what we already believe or wish to believe. Whether we are studying Scripture or ministering to people, curiosity keeps us humble, teachable, and available. Curiosity allows us to "keep in step with the Spirit" (Gal 5:25). It is at the heart of the hermeneutical spiral—being open to having our understanding formed and reformed as we continually explore the text.

Curiosity also reveals our attitude in interpretation. A proper reading attitude is always one of "active puzzle-solving" that is not overly committed to acquiring complete, airtight answers.[5] If we are closed-minded, unable to see our own biases and agendas, and unwilling to admit how easily we can be influenced by factors outside the text, then our attitude needs serious adjustment. Think about the best interviewers, the most interesting people, and the wisest counselors you have encountered. They are all curious people. They are always learning, listening, and asking questions, and yet they are humble enough to admit what they don't know. The one thing every expert in interpretation needs is curiosity. *How curious are you?*

4. Dykstra, *Discovering a Sermon*, 5–7.
5. Fokkelman, *Reading Biblical Narrative*, 206–7.

A Movement toward Redemption

Hermeneutics, homiletics, pastoral care, and counseling share the common foundation of "interpretation," but they also share the common goal of "redemption." The grand story of Scripture is God creating people and redeeming them from sin to be transformed into the image of Jesus Christ (Romans 8). As Donald Capps writes, "the relation between preaching and pastoral counseling is based on the good news of the gospel."[6]

In preaching and pastoral counseling, we are privileged to help in the redemption of God's people by pointing them to the love of God, the Lordship of Christ, the power of the Holy Spirit, and the guidance of the Scriptures, which allows them to reinterpret their lives in light of God's perfect understanding of the world. This redemption is about the exchange of a broken life for the life God intends. It involves moving from seeing things from our own limited vantage point to seeing things from God's universal vantage point, from our intentions to God's intentions. In this continual process, we are invited to move from confusion to clarity, selfishness to service, sinfulness to holiness, and ultimately, from death to life—bridging the gap between our world and the world of God's revealed word. This transformation is often called the "fusion of horizons."[7]

In using hermeneutics as a guide for pastoral counseling, we surrender our temptation to lecture, fix, silence, or "theologize" people's problems. We see people as living and human documents and approach them with the same careful attention we use in approaching the Scriptures. We sit humbly and reverently before the text, ask questions, restrain our biases, explore narratives, labor for true understanding, and look for ways for God's truth to be lived out in practical ways. Most importantly, we give people the permission to be real and help them see their stories, no matter how

---

6. Capps, *Pastoral Counseling and Preaching*, 21.

7. See Osborne, *Hermeneutical Spiral*, 466–71; Vanhoozer, *Is There a Meaning?* 106–8.

conflicted they might be, as part of God's story—and therefore, part of ours as well. Consider:

> Since our stories reveal God, no story is ours alone. All our stories are owned by God and reveal truth; therefore no one has the right to say of his story, "This is too weird, painful, boring, shameful, confusing, or dark; therefore I will bury it." All our stories are meant to be available for the purpose of revealing God and connecting us to one another.[8]

Prayer

God, it is only in you that we find the correct interpretation of all things. Whether in Scripture or in our hurting lives and the lives of those you have entrusted to us, show us your presence and truth. Give us grace and patience as we see through a glass, darkly. Help us find new ways to bridge what often seems like two different worlds of ministry. Keep us from infighting about differences in methodology so we can find the common ground we share in order to be part of your work of redemption.

8. Allender, *To Be Told*, 210.

APPENDIX

Pastoral Counseling Using the Five Steps of Interpretation

A Quick Reference Guide for Pastors

STEP 1: Assess Your Pre-Understanding

- Before your appointment, give God any concerns that are on your mind.
- Review any information or feelings about the counselee or topic of counseling.
- During the appointment, assess whether your thoughts and feelings are helping or harming.
- After the appointment, think and pray about these thoughts and feelings.

STEP 2: Listen Intentionally

- Try to understand what the person means, not just what they say.
- Ask the meaning of words, feelings, and gestures that you do not understand.
- Watch what the person's body language is saying. Be aware of your own body language.
- What are the counselee's embedded beliefs about themselves, God, and the world?

STEP 3: Explore History, Culture, and Circumstances

- What about the counselee's past influences his or her current thoughts or feelings?

- Make note of the differences between you and your counselee.

- Be accepting of differences and focus on understanding, not agreement.

- Are you noticing any patterns or coding in the person's life, personality, or issues?

Spend over 50 Percent of Your Time on Steps 1–3

STEP 4: Attempt to Form the Big Idea of the Story

- Build the person's story in your mind using the key elements of narratives.

- What is the person's main conflict? Is it personal, inter-personal, or extra-personal?

- What is the Big Idea of the story: What happens when . . . ?

- Ask questions to help begin re-shaping, re-casting, re-framing, and re-scripting.

STEP 5: Suggest and Ask about Implications and Applications

- Work with the counselee to find what Timeless Truth speaks to their Big Idea.

- Ask the counselee what applications they can begin to see, given this Timeless Truth.

- What possible barriers does the counselee see to their thinking, actions, and feelings?

- Work together to create a plan that will encourage steady and lasting change.

Bibliography

Adams, Jay Edward. *The Use of the Scriptures in Counseling*. Nutley, NJ: Presbyterian and Reformed, 1975.

Allender, Dan B. *To Be Told: Know Your Story, Shape Your Life*. Colorado Springs: Waterbrook, 2005.

Barnes, M. Craig. *The Pastor as Minor Poet*. Grand Rapids: Eerdmans, 2009.

Boisen, Anton T. "The Living Human Document." In *Images of Pastoral Care: Classic Readings*, edited by Robert C. Dykstra, 22–29. Chalice: Saint Louis, 2005.

Bonhoeffer, Dietrich. *A Testament to Freedom: The Essential Writings of Dietrich Bonhoeffer*. Edited by Geffrey B. Kelly and F. Burton Nelson. San Francisco: HarperSanFrancisco, 1995.

Capps, Donald. *Deadly Sins and Saving Virtues*. Eugene, OR: Wipf and Stock, 2000.

———. *Pastoral Counseling and Preaching: A Quest for an Integrated Ministry*. Eugene, OR: Wipf and Stock, 2003.

Carson, D. A. *Exegetical Fallacies*. Grand Rapids: Baker, 1996.

Chapman, Gary D. *The Five Love Languages: The Secret to Love that Lasts*. Chicago: Northfield, 2010. http://www.5lovelanguages.com.

Clinton, Timothy E., and Mark R. Laaser. *The Quick-Reference to Sexuality and Relationship Counseling*. Grand Rapids: Baker, 2010.

Clinton, Timothy E., and Diane Langberg. *The Quick-Reference Guide to Counseling Women*. Grand Rapids: Baker, 2011.

Clinton, Timothy E., and John Trent. *The Quick-Reference Guide to Marriage and Family Counseling*. Grand Rapids: Baker, 2009.

Clinton, Timothy E., and Ronald E. Hawkins. *The Quick-Reference Guide to Biblical Counseling: Personal and Emotional Issues*. Grand Rapids: Baker, 2009.

Coleson, Joseph E., ed. *Treasure the Word: A Layperson's Guide to Interpreting Scripture*. Wesleyan Theological Perspectives. Indianapolis: Wesleyan, 2009.

Cusick, Jason. "The Clown: Toward a Metaphor for Chaplaincy in the Postmodern Hospital." *Chaplaincy Today* 21 (2005) 12–18.

Dinkins, Burrell David. *Narrative Pastoral Counseling*. Maitland, FL: Xulon, 2005.

Bibliography

Doehring, Carrie. *The Practice of Pastoral Care: A Postmodern Approach.* Louisville: Westminster John Knox, 2006.

Dykstra, Robert C. *Discovering a Sermon: Personal Pastoral Preaching.* Saint Louis: Chalice, 2001.

Edwards, J. Kent. *Effective First-Person Biblical Preaching: The Steps from Text to Sermon.* Grand Rapids: Zondervan, 2005.

———. "Stories Are for Adults." *Preaching Today.* February 19, 2007, accessed January 20, 2012. http://www.preachingtoday.com/skills/themes/stories/storiesareforadults.html.

Erickson, Erik Homburger. *Identity and the Life Cycle.* Norton: New York, 1994.

Fairchild, David. "Exegeting vs. Eisogeting People." March 22, 2007, accessed Febuary 24, 2011. http://www.pastorfairchild.com/2007-03/22/exegeting-vs-eisogeting-people.

Fee, Gordon D. *Paul's Letter to the Philippians.* New International Commentary on the New Testament. Grand Rapids: Eerdmans, 1995.

Ferguson, Duncan S. *Biblical Hermeneutics: An Introduction.* Atlanta: John Knox, 1986.

Ferguson, Sheri S. "Clergy Compassion Fatigue." *Family Therapy Magazine* 2 (2007) 16–19.

Fokkelman, J. P. *Reading Biblical Narrative: An Introductory Guide.* Louisville: Westminster John Knox, 2000.

Geertz, Clifford. *The Interpretation of Cultures.* New York: Basic, 1973.

Gerkin, Charles V. *The Living Human Document: Re-visioning Pastoral Counseling in a Hermeneutical Mode.* Nashville: Abingdon, 1984.

Gibson, Scott M. "Don't Turn Exegesis into an Autopsy." *Preaching Points* 230. Podcast audio. Haddon W. Robinson Center for Preaching at Gordon-Conwell Theological Seminary. MP3, 5:17. August 6, 2009. https://itunes.apple.com/us/podcast/dont-turn-exegesis-into-autopsy/id428971635?i=92525335&mt=2.

Gibson, Scott M., and Jeff Arthurs. "The Mood Isn't Always Imperative." *Preaching Points* 227. Podcast audio. Haddon W. Robinson Center for Preaching at Gordon-Conwell Theological Seminary. MP3, 4:48. August 6, 2009. https://itunes.apple.com/us/podcast/making-mood-fit-message/id428971635?i=92525354&mt=2.

Glenn, Cheryl, and Krista Ratcliffe, eds. *Silence and Listening as Rhetorical Arts.* Carbondale: Southern Illinois University Press, 2011.

Green, Joel B., and Michael Pasquarello III, eds. *Narrative Reading, Narrative Preaching: Reuniting New Testament Interpretation and Proclamation.* Grand Rapid: Baker, 2003.

Guthrie, George H. *Read the Bible for Life: Your Guide to Understanding and Living God's Word.* Nashville: Broadman and Holman, 2011.

Haugk, Kenneth C. *Christian Caregiving: A Way of Life.* Minneapolis: Augsburg, 1984.

Ibarra, Herminia, and Kent Lineback. "What's Your Story?" In *Harvard Business Review on Managing Yourself,* 43–61. Harvard Business Review Paperback Series. Boston: Harvard, 2005.

Kaiser, Walter C., Jr. "A Principilizing Model." In *Four Views on Moving Beyond the Bible to Theology*, edited by Gary T. Meadors and Stanley N. Gundry, 19–50. Counterpoints. Grand Rapids: Zondervan, 2009.

Keller, Timothy. "Timothy Keller on How He Prepares Sermons." *Preaching Today*. November 23, 2009, accessed September 21, 2010. http://www.preachingtoday.com/skills/2009/november/timkelleronhowhe-preparessermons.html.

Killen, James L., Jr. *Pastoral Care in the Small Membership Church*. Abingdon: Nashville, 2005.

Klein, William W., et al. *Introduction to Biblical Interpretation*. Dallas: Word, 1993.

Kollar, Charles Allen. *Solution-Focused Pastoral Counseling: An Effective Short-Term Approach for Getting People Back on Track*. Grand Rapids: Zondervan, 1997.

Köstenberger, Andreas J., and Richard Duane Patterson. *Invitation to Biblical Interpretation: Exploring the Hermeneutical Triad of History, Literature, and Theology*. Invitation to Theological Studies. Grand Rapids: Kregel, 2011.

Kraft, Charles H. *Christianity in Culture: A Study in Dynamic Biblical Theologizing in Cross-Cultural Perspective*. Maryknoll: Orbis, 2005.

Kuruvilla, Abraham. "Pericopes, Theology, and Application." In *Privilege the Text! A Theological Hermeneutic for Preaching*, 89–134. Chicago: Moody, 2013.

Life Innovations, Inc. "Overview of Prepare/Enrich." *Prepare/Enrich*. https://www.prepare-enrich.com.

Lingenfelter, Sherwood G., and Marvin Keene Mayers. *Ministering Cross-Culturally: An Incarnational Model for Personal Relationships*. Grand Rapids: Baker, 2003.

Long, Thomas G. *Preaching and the Literary Forms of the Bible*. Philadelphia: Fortress, 1989.

———. *Preaching from Memory to Hope*. Lyman Beecher Lectures at Yale, 2006. Louisville: Westminster John Knox, 2009.

Mack, Wayne A. "Developing a Helping Relationship with Counselees." In *Introduction to Biblical Counseling*, edited by John F. MacArthur et al., 173–88. Dallas: Word, 1994.

———. "Taking Counselee Inventory: Collecting Data." In *Introduction to Biblical Counseling*, edited by John F. MacArthur et al., 210–30. Dallas: Word, 1994.

Mathews, Alice P. *Preaching That Speaks to Women*. Grand Rapids: Baker, 2003.

McCartney, Dan, and Charles Clayton. *Let the Reader Understand: A Guide to Interpreting and Applying the Bible*. Philipsburg, NJ: Presbyterian and Reformed, 2002.

McKee, Robert. *Story: Substance, Structure, Style and the Principles of Screenwriting*. New York: HarperCollins, 1997.

Moo, Douglas J. "'Flesh' in Romans: A Challenge for the Translator." In *The Challenge of Bible Translation: Communicating God's Word to the World; Essays in Honor of Ronald F. Youngblood,* edited by Glen G. Scorgie, Mark L. Strauss, and Steven M. Voth, 365–80. Grand Rapids: Zondervan, 2003.

Navarro, Joe. *What Every Body Is Saying: An Ex-FBI Agent's Guide to Speed-Reading People.* New York: HarperCollins, 2008.

Nebeker, Gary. "'Who Packed Your Bags?': Factors That Influence Our Preunderstandings." *Bible.org.* October 11, 2004. www.bible.org/article/"who-packed-your-bags"-factors-influence-our-preunderstandings.

Nouwen, Henri J. M. *The Wounded Healer: Ministry in Contemporary Society.* Garden City, NY: Image, 1972.

Osborne, Grant R. *The Hermeneutical Spiral: A Comprehensive Introduction to Biblical Interpretation.* 2nd ed. Downers Grove, IL: InterVarsity, 2006.

Payne, Martin. *Narrative Therapy: An Introduction for Counsellors.* London: Sage, 2006.

Perspectives Study Program. "Course Overview." *Perspectives on the World Christian Movement.* http://www.perspectives.org/About#/HTML/course_overview.htm.

Petersen, Bruce L. *Foundations of Pastoral Care.* Kansas City, MO: Beacon Hill, 2007.

Pratt, Richard L. *He Gave Us Stories: The Bible Student's Guide to Interpreting Old Testament Narratives.* Philipsburg, NJ: Presbyterian and Reformed, 1993.

Pruyser, Paul W. *The Minister as Diagnostician: Personal Problems in Pastoral Perspective.* Philadelphia: Westminster, 1976.

Ralston, Timothy J. "Showing the Relevance: Application, Ethics, and Preaching." In *Interpreting the New Testament Text: Introduction to the Art and Science of Exegesis,* edited by Darrell L. Bock and Buist M. Fanning, 293–310. Wheaton, IL: Crossway, 2006.

Richards, E. Randolph, and Brandon J. O'Brien. *Misreading Scripture with Western Eyes: Removing Cultural Blinders to Better Understand the Bible.* Downers Grove, IL: InterVarsity, 2012.

Robinson, Haddon W. *Biblical Preaching: The Development and Delivery of Expository Messages.* Grand Rapids: Baker, 2001.

Robinson, Haddon W., Jeff Arthurs, and Scott M. Gibson. "Preach through Painful Experiences." *Preaching Points 193.* Podcast audio. Haddon W. Robinson Center for Preaching at Gordon-Conwell Theological Seminary. MP3, 5:58. March 8, 2010. https://itunes.apple.com/us/podcast/preach-through-painful-experiences/id428971635?i=92525357&mt=2.

Scholes, Robert. *Textual Power: Literary Theory and the Teaching of English.* New Haven: Yale University Press, 1985.

Shields, Harry, and Gary J. Bredfeldt. *Caring for Souls: Counseling under the Authority of Scripture.* Moody: Chicago, 2001.

Smith, James Bryan. *The Good and Beautiful God: Falling in Love with the God Jesus Knows*. Apprentice Series. Downers Grove: InterVarsity, 2009.

Sunukjian, Donald. *Invitation to Biblical Preaching: Proclaiming Truth With Clarity and Relevance*. Invitation to Theological Studies 2. Grand Rapids: Kregel, 2007.

Terry, Milton Spenser. *Biblical Hermeneutics: A Treatise on the Interpretation of the Old and New Testaments*. Eugene, OR: Wipf and Stock, 1999.

Townsend, John. *Leadership Beyond Reason: How Great Leaders Succeed by Harnessing the Power of Their Values, Feelings, and Intuition*. Nelson: Nashville, 2009.

Vanhoozer, Kevin J. "A Drama-of-Redemption Model." In *Four Views on Moving Beyond the Bible to Theology*, edited by Gary T. Meadors and Stanley N. Gundry, 151–99. Counterpoints. Grand Rapids: Zondervan, 2009.

———. *Is There a Meaning in This Text? The Bible, the Reader, and the Morality of Literary Knowledge*. Landmarks in Christian Scholarship. Grand Rapids: Zondervan, 2009.

Vanhoozer, Kevin J., Charles A. Anderson, and Michael J. Sleasman, eds. *Everyday Theology: How to Read Cultural Texts and Interpret Trends*. Cultural Exegesis. Grand Rapids: Baker, 2007.

Virkler, Henry A. *Hermeneutics: Principles and Processes of Biblical Interpretation*. Grand Rapids: Baker Books, 1997.

Wakefield, Norm. *Between the Words: The Art of Perceptive Listening*. Grand Rapids: Revell, 2002.

Wiseman, Albert L., et al. *Living Your Strengths: Discover Your God-given Talents and Inspire Your Community*. 3rd ed. New York: Gallup, 2008.

White, Michael, and David Epston. *Narrative Means to Therapeutic Ends*. Norton Professional Books. New York: Norton, 1990.

Wright, John W. *Telling God's Story: Narrative Preaching for Christian Formation*. Downers Grove: InterVarsity, 2007.

Wright, N. T. *Acts, Romans, 1 Corinthians*. Vol. 10 of *The New Interpreter's Bible*. Nashville: Abingdon, 2002.

Made in the USA
San Bernardino, CA
24 October 2014